RAD
BOARDS

RAD
BOARDS

RON KING

A *Sports Illustrated For Kids* Book

First Edition

Library of Congress Cataloging-in-Publication Data

King, Ron.
    Rad boards : skateboarding, snowboarding, bodyboarding, a total
guide to the cutting edge / Ron King. — 1st ed.
        p. cm.
    "A Sports illustrated for kids book."
    Summary: Describes the equipment, techniques, tricks,
competitions, and other aspects of skateboarding, snowboarding, and
bodyboarding.
    ISBN 0-316-49354-6 (hc)
    ISBN 0-316-49355-4 (pb)
    1. Skateboarding—Juvenile literature. 2. Snowboarding—Juvenile
literature. 3. Surfing—Juvenile literature. [1. Skateboarding.
2. Snowboarding. 3. Surfing.] I. Title.
GV859.8K56 1991
796.2'1—dc20   90-46472

SPORTS ILLUSTRATED FOR KIDS is a trademark of
THE TIME INC. MAGAZINE COMPANY.

Sports Illustrated For Kids Books is a joint imprint of Little,
Brown and Company and Warner Juvenile Books and is
published in arrangement with Cloverdale Press Inc.

10 9 8 7 6 5 4 3 2 1

KP

For further information regarding this title, write to Little,
Brown and Company, 34 Beacon Street, Boston, MA 02108

Published simultaneously in Canada by Little, Brown & Company
(Canada) Limited

Printed in the United States of America

Interior design by Harold Nolan
Interior illustrations by Jackie Aher

To Gertrude Crosland King, for years of unswerving support

My deepest thanks to Bill Dellefield of Body Boarding magazine, who tirelessly coached me through learning some of the finer details of his sport; to Jay Cabler of SK8 Hut in Knoxville, Tennessee, for his close guidance; Chris Copley of Burton Snowboards; Jake Burton Carpenter, for pioneering the sport of snowboarding for far more than reasons of profit; Lee Crane and Kevin Kinneer of Snowboarding magazine; Don Bostic of the National Skateboard Association; Pat Dugan of BZ Pro Boards, Inc.; Steve Casimiro; and J. David Miller, for inspiration and friendship.

TABLE OF CONTENTS

BODYBOARDING 53

CHAPTER 1

ALL ABOUT RAD BOARDS

Common Ground

Skateboarding, snowboarding and bodyboarding began in different places at different times. In many ways, though, the sports are very much alike. For one thing, in each sport you ride on top of a long, narrow board. The shape of these boards has evolved from the shape of a surfboard, and surfing is the granddaddy of all rad sports.

Rad sports also share a lot of the same language, or jargon. For example, when riders in any of the sports cut back and forth on a mountain, wave or hill, they say they are "shredding." And in skateboarding and snowboarding, people who ride with their right foot forward are called "goofy-footers." Most people ride the opposite way, with their left foot forward. The terms shredding and goofy-foot are examples of jargon.

Something else rad sports have in common is clothing. Kids who do these sports like to wear baggy clothes decorated with bright colors—pink stripes, bright green globs, purple splashes and lots of neon. Faded dark colors are also rad. Wearing the right clothes can say that you are into rad sports.

The most important thing that the best rad riders have in common, though, is safety. They know that rad doesn't mean reckless, and that doing dangerous stunts doesn't make them better boarders. The best skateborders, for example, wear helmets, as well as elbow and knee pads. Without safety gear, they know they could be seriously injured when they fall.

Skateboarders also know that skating on streets with traffic is stupid, and that riding a skateboard while holding onto a car fender—even if you have seen it done in the movies—is not cool. Skateboarders are killed every year trying stunts like this. Don't be stupid!

Good bodyboarders and snowboarders also ride safely. The smartest bodyboarders never go into the water alone, and smart snowboarders obey all the rules at the ski slopes.

If you use caution and common sense, you will discover that skateboarding, snowboarding and bodyboarding have something else in common: lots and lots of fun! This book is designed to help you get the most out of rad sports. So read it carefully. Learning to do something well in any rad sport is called "getting it wired." So read on. Get it wired! And get rad!

*R*ad. You know what that means. Awesome. Really cool.

But do you know where the word rad came from? Many people say that kids in Southern California created the word. Southern California is also the birthplace of skateboarding, and the kids who rode skateboards there started calling super-cool moves "radical." This was soon shortened to "rad."

Today, there are a lot of rad sports and rad things you can do. Two other sports that are definitely rad are bodyboarding and snowboarding. Some of the moves you can do in these sports are a lot like moves you can do on a skateboard.

One rad move on a snowboard, for example, is called a "180." To do a 180, you ride a snowboard up a curved wall of snow in what's known as a half-pipe. You fly off the top edge of the wall and into the air. While you are in the air, you spin halfway around, or 180 degrees, so that you are facing back down toward the snow ramp. Then you come back down, land on the ramp and ride down the wall. This is just like a 180 on a skateboard, except that you do it on a snow half-pipe instead of on a plywood half-pipe.

THE BIRTH OF RAD SPORTS

Breaking Waves

Rad sports began hundreds of years ago in the Hawaiian Islands. The Polynesian people who lived there loved to stand on long wooden boards and ride the waves. These people were the world's first surfers. The sport was so popular back then that kings and other nobility would go to the beach and bet on which surfers could ride the waves best. In the 1770s, a British explorer named Captain James Cook landed on Hawaii, and he became the first outsider to see people surfing. At that time, the Polynesians had been surfing for about 100 years.

In the 1800s, Christian missionaries arrived in Hawaii, and they banned surfing. The native Hawaiians continued to ride the waves in outrigger canoes, but surfing was almost forgotten until the 20th century.

Modern surfing really began in the 1950s when a California college student named Robert Simmons made the first fiberglass surfboard. Simmons's board was lighter and easier to maneuver than the old wooden boards. Shortly after that, another Califor-

nia student developed the wetsuit, which kept surfers warm while they waited for waves in the cold Pacific Ocean. A wetsuit is made of a type of rubber called neoprene, and it fits over the body like a glove. It works by allowing a thin layer of water in between the body and the wetsuit. Body heat warms the water, and this keeps the person warm.

With wetsuits and fiberglass boards, it became easier to surf in cold water and challenging waves. Surfing was no longer limited to a few beaches, and its popularity spread quickly. Surfers started appearing in movies. Rock 'n' roll bands like the Beach Boys sang songs about surfing. People were soon riding waves on both coasts of the United States, and even in foreign countries such as Australia, where the waves rolled perfectly onto beautiful beaches.

Because of surfing's renewed popularity, a sport called bellyboarding was also revived. Bellyboards were nothing more than short surfboards that you rode while lying on your stomach. The Polynesians rode crude wooden bellyboards, which they called *paipo* boards.

In the 1970s, though, a new kind of bellyboard was developed. Unlike surfboards, which were made of fiberglass, the new bellyboards were made of foam. The foam was flexible and could be bent to help you steer. The foam was also soft, so the board didn't hurt when it hit you in the head. These rad boards became known as bodyboards. In the 1980s, bodyboarding became the cool thing to do on a hot summer day at the beach.

Surfing Takes to the Pavement

At about the same time that the surfing craze was spreading across the country, another rad sport was being created. This sport was a lot like surfing, except that it was done on pavement, using a board with wheels on the bottom. The sport became known as sidewalk surfing, or skateboarding.

Kids began nailing roller skate wheels to boards in the 1950s, but the modern era of skateboarding began in the 1960s when a few small companies in Southern California began making and selling skateboards. At first, skateboards were sold in surfing shops, and surfers bought them to ride on days when they couldn't ride the waves.

Soon, however, skateboards were being sold in toy stores and sporting good stores, and kids who had never even seen a surfboard were zipping down the street on sidewalk surfboards. The first skateboards were stiff and hard to turn, so skaters couldn't do many of the tricks that are popular today. But skateboarding was still a lot of fun. Soon there were contests. Skateboard companies grew. And skateboarders appeared on the covers of national magazines.

In the late 1960s, though, skateboarding almost died. Newspaper and magazines began publishing stories about how skateboarding caused broken bones and concussions. Doctors warned parents not to let their kids ride skateboards. Some towns even made skateboarding illegal.

Part of the problem was that the first skateboards used metal wheels. These wheels slid on sharp corners, and they stopped suddenly when they hit a pebble or a bump.

The sport was finally revived when Frank Nasworthy developed wheels made of a plastic called polyurethane. These wheels gripped the pavement and ran smoothly over small bumps. Skateboards became safer, and the sport became hot again. In the 1980s, skateboarding really boomed. Its popularity spread across the country, and it even became rad in Europe, Australia, Japan and other foreign countries. Today, it's hard to go anywhere in the modern world and not see kids riding skateboards.

Snow, the Last Frontier

As the popularity of surfing and skateboarding grew, an inventor named Sherman Poppen began thinking of ways to ride a board on snow. Poppen worked for a company that made bowling equipment, and he knew how to work with wood to build bowling alleys.

He used this knowledge to make the first snowboard. He called his board a Snurfer, a word that came from a combination of "snow" and "surfer."

Snurfers were made out of plywood and were steered by a rope attached to the nose. Poppen's company, the Brunswick Sporting Goods Company, sold more than a million Snurfers. But Snurfering was merely a fad that disappeared after a couple of years.

The idea of riding a board on snow was kept alive by two other board riders. In New Jersey, skateboarder Tom Sims wanted to create a board that he could ride in the winter. At about the same time, a surfer named Jake Burton from Long Island, New York, began tinkering with the Snurfer. Burton wanted to build a Snurfer that turned better.

Eventually, both Sims and Burton developed a snowboard that resembled a short, wide ski. They glued strips of wood together to form the core, and they covered the top and bottom of the core with layers of plastic. On the edges, they attached strips of metal, which would cut through hard, icy snow.

Sims and Burton launched a craze. The new snowboards were much easier to turn and rode a lot more smoothly than the old Snurfers. Many skateboarders loved snowboarding because it let them ride in the winter. Many skiers switched to snowboarding because it was a different and exciting sport.

Hundreds, then thousands of snowboarders began showing up at ski slopes all over the country. Almost immediately, though, this created problems. Ski slopes were perfect for snowboarding, but many skiers didn't like sharing their mountains. People who ran the ski slopes were afraid that snowboarders would crash into skiers and frighten them away. Many ski resorts banned snowboards, and it took a few years before skiers and snowboarders learned that they could safely slide down a mountain side by side.

Today, most ski resorts allow snowboards, and Jake Burton deserves a lot of credit for the sport's acceptance. He distributed videos of snowboarding, visited ski areas to ask permission for snowboarders to use the ski hills, and formed a team of experts to give snowboarding demonstrations.

Rad Sports Go Belly Down

waves. And a bodyboard doesn't hurt when it conks you on the head.

Today, bodyboarding is a highly visible and competitive sport. Mike Stewart, the sport's superstar, has won more than $75,000 in bodyboarding contests. But money isn't the reason to try bodyboarding. You should try riding the waves because it's fun. You'll learn more about this sport in the bodyboarding section of this book.

While Burton and Sims were perfecting their snowboards, a Southern California inventor and surfer named Tom Morey was tinkering with a new kind of surfboard. Morey wanted to make a bellyboard out of soft foam. In the early 1970s, he started making boards out of polyethylene, which feels like hard foam rubber. Morey called these bodyboards, and he began selling them through the mail and out of his workshop in Carlsbad, California.

Other small companies soon began making bodyboards. Competitions were held to test bodyboarders' skills. A magazine devoted to the sport was launched. Soon, there were bodyboards for beginners and boards for experts, boards for small waves and boards for big waves. Today, there are more than 100 kinds of bodyboards to chose from. Some of the most popular are the Morey Boogie brand, named after the inventor of the board. Other major manufacturers include Easy Rider, BZ and Turbo.

Bodyboarding has become popular because it's fun and because it's easier to learn than surfing. Bodyboards also cost about a quarter as much as surfboards. They are often permitted at beaches that ban surfboards. A bodyboard can be ridden on small

State of the Art

As you can see, the history of rad sports is linked to inventions and new technology. As inventors made skateboards, snowboards and bodyboards better and easier to use, more and more people started riding them. All the improvements have made rad sports safer and a lot more fun. But that doesn't mean you can do anything you want on a rad board. Even the pros who do the wildest tricks are very careful and follow the rules. As you read the next chapter on board design, keep safety in mind. You shouldn't try every trick you see someone else do. Learn the easy moves, and then move on to the harder stuff.

Boards, gnarly moves, jargon, and style—these are some of the things rad boards have in common. But skateboarding, snowboarding and bodyboarding are also very different, and each has its own gear, its own moves—and its own awesome challenges.

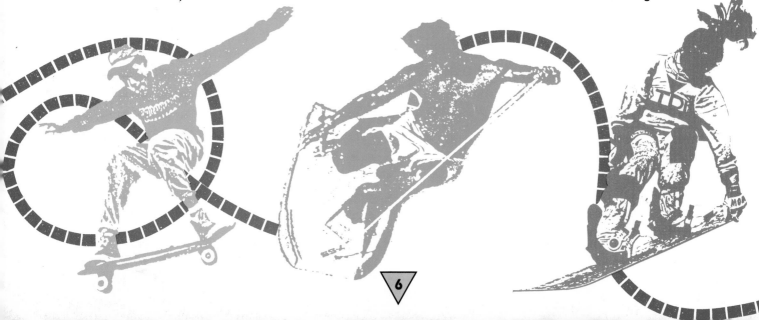

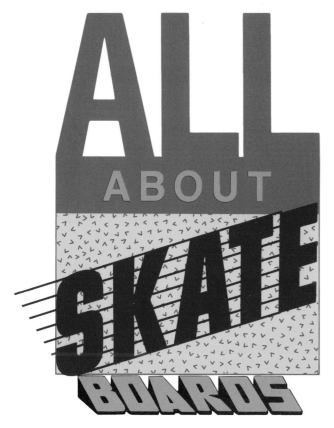

ALL ABOUT SKATE BOARDS

O ver the years, skateboards have changed shape radically. In the 1960s and 1970s, skateboards were smaller than they are today and they had sharper noses. They looked more like surfboards back then. Today's skateboard is wider and longer and has a stubbier nose and tail. The nose is the front of the board, and the tail is the back. The deck is the board itself.

Materials that skateboards are made from have changed, too. Old boards were made out of fiberglass, wood and aluminum. The best skateboards today are made of wood—layers of Canadian hard maple glued together. Boards that are glued together are called laminated boards. Skaters have discovered that laminated maple boards are strong and light in weight.

A good board is also scooped out on top so your feet stay in place, and the nose and tail are turned up. Of course, there is more to a skateboard than just the board itself. In addition to the deck, there are two other major parts: the trucks and the wheels. The trucks are the long metal pieces on the bottom of the board that hold the wheels. When you buy a skateboard, you need to select a deck, wheels and trucks that fit the style of skateboarding you plan to do.

Skating Styles

There are three styles of skateboarding. Ramp skaters go up and down ramps at high speeds and perform tricks. Street skaters ride on sidewalks and streets. Freestyle skaters are a combination of the two: They do tricks, but on sidewalks and streets. Freestylers do things like spinning around on the back wheels and standing the board on end.

Just as there are three ways to skate, there are also three basic kinds of skateboards. But before you decide which kind to buy, you have another decision to make first: whether to purchase a board, wheels and trucks already assembled, or to buy the parts separately and assemble the board yourself.

Ready-made boards are cheaper: They usually cost from $80 to $100. Custom-made boards cost about $120 to $160. If you're just starting, it's best to buy a ready-made board. You probably won't know exactly what kind of board you want until after you have ridden for awhile.

If you do want to buy the parts separately, you have some complicated choices ahead of you. For instance, if you plan to ride your board mostly on ramps, then you need a big board with tall wheels and wide trucks. A ramp board is usually about one inch longer and a half-inch wider than a street board. This makes the board more stable, which is important because most people ride boards faster on ramps than they do on the street.

Trucks and Wheels

As well as being a little bit bigger, ramp skateboards also have wider trucks than street or freestyle skateboards. They also have wheels that are bigger and made of harder plastic.

The trucks on a ramp board are about a half-inch wider than street trucks. Wider trucks give ramp boards more stability. This is important when you're riding up the vertical wall of a ramp at high speeds!

The wheels on a ramp skateboard are usually 66 to 68 millimeters, or about 2½ inches, high (wheels are not measured in inches but in millimeters). Tall wheels make a skateboard roll faster than short wheels. You want a faster wheel for ramps so that you will have the speed to roll up that ramp wall.

Ramp wheels are also very hard, which makes them roll faster. If you take a rubber ball and press it against the ground, it loses its shape and turns flat on one side. Since the ball is no longer round, it's not going to roll very fast because it has more of what's called "rolling resistance." The same thing happens to plastic skateboard wheels when you add your weight to the deck—even though you can't really see it with your naked eye. A harder wheel doesn't flatten as much when you stand on the board. Because it has less of its surface in contact with the ground, the wheel has less rolling resistance. Therefore it rolls faster.

Wheel hardness is measured on the Durometer Scale, which uses the letter A. The softest wheel is 85A. The hardest is 98A. Ramp riders generally like a 97A or 98A wheel.

If you plan to ride your board mostly on streets and sidewalks, then you want a different kind of skateboard. Street boards are slightly smaller and have short, soft wheels and narrow trucks. This kind of board lets you maneuver much more quickly to dodge obstacles—and there are lots of those to look out for on sidewalks and streets! Street wheels are usually about a 90A on the Durometer Scale. Becaues they're softer, they give you a much smoother ride over small pebbles and pavement cracks. Similarly, street wheels are about 58 to 60 millimeters tall, or about a quarter-inch shorter than ramp wheels. Trucks on street boards will be about a half-inch narrower than ramp trucks.

Freestyle skateboards are the smallest and the easiest to maneuver. They're one or two inches shorter than street boards, and the trucks are about one-and-a-half inches narrower. Freestyle wheels are about 55 to 60 millimeters high, but they are very hard. This gives the wheels both maneuverability and speed.

Dressed to grab air! Wearing helmets, knee pads and elbow pads—these skateboarders know it takes more than gnarly decals to skate safely.

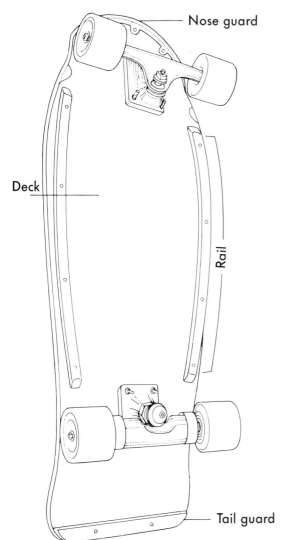

Nose guard

Deck

Rail

Tail guard

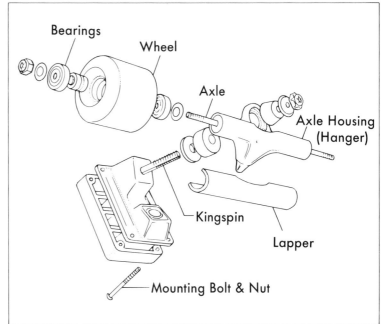

Bearings

Wheel

Axle

Axle Housing
(Hanger)

Kingspin

Lapper

Mounting Bolt & Nut

A typical skateboard, truck and wheels. The best skateboards are made of laminated maple wood.

Board Sizes

Once you've decided which kind of riding style and skateboard is right for you, you need to select a board that's the proper length. This is easy. Look at the top of the deck. You should see the heads of eight bolts that attach the trucks to the deck. There are four bolts in the front and four in the back. Stand sideways on the board with one foot just behind each set of bolts. Your feet should be about shoulder-width apart. If they feel too far apart or too close together, get a shorter or longer board.

If you're shorter than 5'6", get a street or "mini" board. These are no more than 30 inches long. If you're taller than 5'6", you have your choice of all three boards: street, ramp or vertical.

Where to Buy

If you're confused by all these choices, the best thing to do is to visit a good shop. The best skateboard shops sell nothing but skateboards and accessories, and a salesperson will help you find a board that's perfect for you.

CHAPTER 4

N ow that you have a skateboard, you're ready to roll! If you're a beginner, though, don't be in too much of a hurry to do the hot moves. You need to learn the basic skills before going on to the fancy tricks.

The best way to start is to find a friend who already knows how to skate. He or she can show you the basics, such as pushing off, turning and stopping. For your first try, start on flat, smooth pavement such as an empty parking lot. Stay away from streets and sidewalks for the time being. And save the ramps for much later.

As for clothes, be sure to wear something loose and comfortable; a t-shirt, baggy shorts and sneakers are the usual gear.

And don't forget your pads and helmet! If you don't wear safety gear, your days as a rad skater may be numbered.

With that settled, let's start with a few fundamentals.

The Stance

The first thing to learn is where to put your feet. Most people stand on a skateboard with their left foot for-

ward. Putting the right foot forward is called the ''goofy-foot'' position. You should stand whichever way is most comfortable.

Before you stand on the board for the first time, find a fence or a friend to hold on to for balance. Put your front foot on the board, then the back foot. Remember to put each foot just behind the bolts. You should be standing sideways. Relax. Now turn your front foot just a little more forward than your rear foot, which should be sideways on the board. Bend slightly at the knees and waist, lift your arms and bend the elbows. Keep most of your weight on your front foot.

This is the basic stance. It's the same position used by the best skaters in the world, dudes like Christian Hosoi, Danny Way and Steve Caballero, who are all ranked in the top 10 of American skaters in ramp and street styles. While you're trying out your stance, flex your ankles forward and back a few times to get a feel for turning the board. Now you're ready to start riding!

Pushing Off

Now comes the big moment. While holding on to the fence or to your friend for support, take your rear foot off the board and put it on the ground behind you. Very slowly, push yourself forward with that foot. Then put the foot back on the deck and immediately get into your basic stance—arms up, waist, knees and elbows bent.

Take it slow. Get used to the movement before trying to go too fast. Experiment with the basic stance by exaggerating the bend in your knees and waist and getting into a deeper crouch. By doing this, you'll eventually find the position that gives you maximum stability.

Your front foot is your stabilizing foot. You guide the board with just that foot. If you want a little insurance at the beginning, you can keep your rear foot hovering just above the ground instead of putting it back on the board. That way, if you feel shaky, you can set that foot down and brace yourself. You can also use that foot to give yourself another push. Remember to keep your weight forward.

Stopping

Obviously, this is one of the most important moves to learn. There are several ways to stop on a skateboard. One is to use the rear foot as a brake. To do this, put all your weight on your front foot and then gently tap the toes of your rear foot on the ground several times. That will slow you down!

This skater has just pushed off in the "goofy-foot" position —with his right foot forward on the board.

Another way to stop—especially in an emergency situation—is to jump off the board and run. Make sure you jump forward and out to the side to avoid the board. And make sure that you hit the ground running as fast as the board is rolling. Otherwise, you could fly head over heels to a hard landing.

These ways of stopping are O.K. at low speeds, but don't use either when you're going fast. To make a high-speed stop, you'll need to learn a "front-side slide." But before you learn this stunt, you have one more lesson ahead of you—how to fall down!

Sorry, dude! If you're going to get wired, it's impossible not to fall down sometimes. Every skater falls—even Tony Hawk, who is probably the best skateboarder in the world. Tony can do tricks on a ramp that no other skater alive can do. But you know what? Tony falls dozens of times a day trying to learn new tricks. So learn how to handle a fall like a pro.

Believe it or not, falling is something you should practice. As Tony Hawk says, "falling is an acquired skill." That means the better you are at falling, the less your chances of getting hurt when you do fall. The first thing to remember about falling is to relax! You're more likely to hurt yourself if you stiffen up. Always try to anticipate a fall before it happens, and concentrate on staying loose. Roll with the fall as much as you can.

Whatever you do, avoid reaching out with your hands and arms to break your fall. This is how skateboarders sprain or break their wrists. It's hard to resist the instinct to use your hands, though. Tony Hawk advises beginners and intermediate skaters to wear wrist guards. After all, if you break your wrist, you won't be able to skateboard again for a long time.

Also make sure you're wearing the rest of your safety gear. When you practice falling, simply put on your helmet, gloves, knee and elbow pads, and go out to a grassy yard. In most cases, the safest fall is either a "knee slide" or a "body roll." You'll probably fall hundreds of times in your skating career. These moves can keep you from getting hurt.

The Knee Slide

The knee slide is the standard fall when you're skateboarding at high speed on half-pipes and other ramps.

It's not as safe on pavement where a rough surface prevents you from sliding smoothly. To do a knee slide, you must anticipate a fall. As you lose your balance, step off the board, take one or two quick steps forward on the ground, and then fall forward and land on your knee pads. Tuck your feet beneath you with your toes pointing backward. Don't use your hands. If you fall forward, land on your elbow pads. Remember—practice this a few times on a lawn before doing it on a hard surface.

The Body Roll

Next you're ready to practice falling backward. Be careful because there's no completely safe way to fall backward. One solution is to turn around quickly and do a knee slide. But if you don't have time for that, try doing a body roll. Never fall flat on your back.

To practice falling backward the right way, take a few fast steps as if you're getting ready to do a cartwheel. Then tuck your shoulder and do a sideways somersault. When your back hits the ground, roll across it diagonally from one shoulder to the opposite hip. That will spread out the impact over a larger area of your body.

Practice this many times, slowly and carefully. You need to be so good at it that you don't even have to think before doing it. You might try a few falls on a gym mat or an old mattress.

Now for the good news about falling backward—as you get better and better at skateboarding, you'll do it less and less often. Those kinds of tumbles almost never happen to pros like Tony Hawk and Christian Hosoi.

The Back-Side Turn

When you've learned to fall properly, you're ready to work on turns. First, find a gentle slope that's clear of rocks, straw, dirt and other debris. That way, you won't have to worry about dodging obstacles.

Start with a "back-side" turn. It's called that because your back is turned into the direction you're skating. For regular-footed riders, this is a turn to the right. (All directions here are for regular-footers, or people who stand with their left foot forward. If you put your right foot forward, simply do the opposite—start, for example, with a left turn, which is a back-side turn for goofy-footers.)

Begin by pushing off slowly and getting into the basic stance. Then lean forward a bit, pushing your toes down so the board tilts down slightly in the direction you are turning. Use the heel of your rear foot as a brake against the board tilt. Try to look six or eight feet ahead of you, and not at your feet. If you're leaning into the turn, you'll find that the board will follow your upper body through the turn. To stop turning, shift your weight back to the center of the board so that the board levels off.

Simple enough, right? The basic idea is to lead the board through the turn with your body while you tilt the board in the direction of the turn. This is the fundamental concept for any skateboarding turn.

The Front-Side Turn

A front-side turn is pretty much a reverse of a back-side turn. For a regular-footer, start by bending at the waist and tipping your left shoulder back (to about 8:00) and your right shoulder forward (to about 2:00). Your shoulders lead your body in the direction of the turn. As you lean, rock your ankles backward, tilting the deck of the board backward. Again, the board should follow you through the turn. To come out of the turn, shift your weight forward over the center of the board.

Try connecting left and right turns together. As you improve, you'll find yourself developing a natural rhythm. Going into a turn, bend at the waist and knees and put more weight on the forward foot. Coming out of the turn, straighten up a bit and shift your weight back to both feet.

If your board feels unresponsive and stiff, try loosening the trucks. To do this, turn the board over and find the adjustment bolt between each set of wheels. This bolt is called the ''king pin.'' With a wrench, turn the bolts to the left, or counterclockwise, to loosen them. Make sure you loosen both trucks an equal amount. If your board feels like it turns too easily, turn the bolts to the right, or clockwise, to tighten them.

With practice, you can take on steeper hills, making turn after turn smoothly and quickly. Now you're discovering the joy of skateboarding. You're also ready to learn a few tricks.

The front-side turn. In any skateboarding turn, the basic idea is to turn with your body, and let your skate-board follow you.

C H A P T E R   5

EX-CELLENT TRICKS

There are hundreds of skateboard stunts. Many have really rad names like the eggplant, the jolly mamba, the stale fish and the McTwist. Skaters are constantly inventing new tricks and making the old ones fancier. There are so many tricks that no single skateboarder can possibly know them all. Fortunately, many tricks are just variations on a few basic tricks.

The Kick Turn

One basic move is the kick turn, which is simply a quicker, sharper version of the regular front-side or back-side turn. To do a kick turn, shift your rear foot back toward the tail and lift your front foot a few inches to let the nose float off the ground. With most of your weight on the rear foot, spin the board around on its rear wheels by quickly rotating your shoulders, arms and hips into the turn.

You can do either a front-side or a back-side kick turn. And you can do them on a ramp or on flat ground. The key to the kick turn is spinning the board around smoothly on its back wheels. As you progress, you'll learn how to control the board better with your rear foot. At first, work on making a 180-degree kick turn, which will turn the nose halfway around so that you're facing the opposite direction.

As you improve, you will want to try 360-degree turns, which means you spin in a complete circle. Eventually, you may be able turn several circles at once. Some of the best freestylers can make dozens of 360s non-stop.

The Front-Side Slide

Once you've gotten the kick turn wired, it's easy to learn the front-side slide. The front-side slide is not only a good way to stop, but it's also a hot-looking trick. To do one, begin a sharp turn to the left (to the right for goofy-footers). About halfway into the turn, quickly shift most of your weight to the rear foot as you rock back on your heel. As the back end slides around, shift your weight forward to stay centered over the board. If you keep your weight on the back foot, the board will continue to slide around until you are going backward.

If you really stomp the back of the board around, the wheels will screech to a sideways stop. But you don't have to stop the board completely. You can do front-side slides as a sideways skid to make your turns look fancier.

The Ollie

The ollie is one of the most popular tricks in skateboarding. You use an ollie to jump over obstacles on the street or to get some air on a ramp. Often the ollie is simply a way to get your board airborne so that you can do a much fancier trick, such as sliding down a rail.

To do an ollie, start by doing a foot stomp as if you're going to do a kick turn. As the front of the board lifts off the ground, jump up, which lifts the whole board into the air. As soon as you jump, kick the nose back down with your front foot. This levels off the board in mid-air. You should land back on all four wheels, rolling and ready for more.

The ollie isn't an easy trick, but once you've learned it you can hop curbs and other obstacles without stopping to pick up your board and go around. As a publicity stunt, Tony Hawk once ollied over a dumpster trash bin—with the lid open. He started from an elevated platform to give him enough speed to sail above the eight-foot-high bin and across its six-foot opening.

Of course, you shouldn't try something like that. The stunt was very dangerous—Hawk later said it was the scariest thing he's ever done, and that's a champion talking!

Street skaters use the ollie to hop curbs and other obstacles. For ramp and freestyle skaters, the ollie is the start of even more awesome tricks.

Grinds

One of the common tricks in both ramp and street skating is "grinding." To do a grind, you skid your board on one or both of its trucks along the edge of something—a curb, a rail, or the coping of a ramp, which is the concrete border or metal pipe that runs along the top edge. Grinds are hot stuff in skateboarding. The good skaters do them often and long. The record is 19' 8". It was set by Christian Hosoi on a ramp coping in California in 1988.

A grind is like an extended kick turn, and it has three phases. Approach the curb that you are grinding from a slight angle. Just before you reach the curb, stomp on the tail to kick the nose up onto the edge of the curb. With the front of the board on top of the curb and the tail below it, slide along the curb. The hard part is ending the grind. You have to kick the board free by stomping the tail a little and bringing the nose up. As the nose clears the curb, turn quickly to get your skateboard pointed in the direction you want to go.

You can do either a back-side grind or a front-side grind. Skidding on both trucks at once is called a "fifty-fifty." Watch the more experienced skaters grind and ask lots of questions. You'll catch on sooner or later.

The Rock 'n' Roll

A trick that involves some of the same techniques as a grind is the "rock 'n' roll." In this trick, you ride up onto the edge of a curb, ramp or other object so that the board is in a teeter-totter position. The edge of the ramp or curb should support the board on the bottom of the deck between the two wheel sets. After you've balanced the board for a second or two, kick the nose free, just as you do in a grind.

You don't have to turn the board around after you do a rock 'n' roll or other ramp tricks. You can simply skate backward down the ramp after finishing the trick. This is called a "fakie." When you skate backward down the ramp after doing a rock 'n' roll, it's called a fakie rock 'n' roll.

Aerials

"Aerials" are the really cool part of skateboarding. There's nothing like flying into the air with your skateboard under you, doing all kinds of rad twists and turns. It's an awesome feeling. It's also fun to watch the pros do aerials. Hot riders such as Christian Hosoi seem to have jets on their wheels as they leave the earth and fly through the air to incredible heights. Hosoi and Tony

Magnuson share the world record for aerial height. Both have soared to nine and a half feet above a ramp. Rad stuff.

An aerial is like an ollie, except that you lift the board with a hand as you jump. An aerial is generally easier than an ollie. Most aerial tricks are little more than fast kick turns.

Doing an aerial is simply a matter of building up enough speed to get a little air and then letting the board float upwards with you. That's done by bending at the knees and grabbing the board by one of its rails.

You can learn aerials in street skating, but they're much easier on ramps. So let's look at ramp skating next.

Your very first move in ramp skateboarding will be to put on a helmet, gloves, and elbow and knee pads. At some point you're going to fall, and it's important to be prepared for it. Most skateboarders begin ramp skating on what's called a "launch ramp." A launch ramp is a single curved ramp. Many are only a couple of feet high. You can do virtually any of the basic tricks on a launch ramp. Start with the easy ones first. On your first run, skate a little ways up the ramp and do a front-side or a back-side turn on the ramp wall.

A typical quarter-pipe ramp has a sloping curve, some straight up and down vert, and a coping at the top.

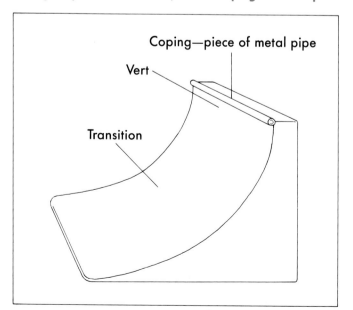

This skater is doing an excellent grind on a super half-pipe. The idea is to skid along the coping as far as you can. The record is almost twenty feet!

Do several more turns, making each one sharper than the previous one. Finally, try a few trick turns on the ramp. As you feel more and more comfortable, start turning higher on the ramp. Eventually, you can graduate to aerials and even grinds on the lip of the ramp. Then you'll be ready to go on to a quarter-pipe. That's where the tricks really get rad.

The Quarter-Pipe

A quarter-pipe looks like a pipe cut lengthwise with the top three-fourths removed. All that's left is the bottom quarter. A half-pipe is like two quarter pipes pushed together. It also has vert, which is an upright section from 12 to 18 inches high at the top of the ramp walls. Save the half-pipes for later. First learn the basic tricks on launch ramps and quarter-pipes.

The first step in skating a quarter-pipe is to learn how to "drop in," or start from the top. Begin by placing the rear wheels and the tail of the board against the coping, which is the metal pipe or strip of smooth concrete built into the top edge of the ramp. Hold the board there by standing on the tail with your rear foot. When you're ready to go, simply place your forward foot on the board and lean forward. This will send you and the board down the wall of the ramp—preferably together. If you fall, do a knee slide and then get up, dust yourself off and try again.

Pumping

When you start skating on a quarter-pipe, try a few kick turns on the wall. Do 180s on both your front side and back side. You'll find that after a couple of these, your board begins to slow down. To keep it going, you have to "pump."

Pumping on a skateboard is like the motion you make on a swing to keep yourself swinging. To pump, flex your knees when you roll to the bottom of the ramp to drop your weight onto the board. Then as you climb the wall, spring upward slightly to unweight the board. You'll discover that pumping on a skateboard comes as easily and naturally as it does on a swingset.

This homemade quarter-pipe has a lot of high vert—all the better to grab air!

20

Getting Air

When you're comfortable doing kick turns, try a few low aerials. Start with wide, gradual turns on the face of a ramp. At the top of each turn, crouch and grab the rail of the board with the hand on the outside of your turn. In other words, if you make a right turn, grab the rail with your left hand. Then spring up, bringing your knees up under you. As you jump, pull the board up to keep it in contact with your feet.

Try turning with a little hop, spinning around as quickly as you can while you're in the air. Take it slow and easy at first. You're bound to fall a few times. Remember to slide on those kneepads.

Eventually you'll be able to sharpen your turns and get more air. Practice both your front-and back-side aerial turns. In no time, you'll be doing 180s. You'll need to pump to get your speed up for them. Then you can start turning higher and higher up the ramp until you're turning near the coping.

Advanced Ramp Skating

Of course, you don't have to turn at all to do an aerial on a quarter-pipe. Instead, you can just get some air and then do a "fakie" back down the ramp. You'll have to practice skating backwards to do this. Be sure to turn your head and shoulders to look in back of you to see where you're going. When you've gotten some of the basic tricks wired on a quarter-pipe, you'll be ready for a half-pipe.

The half-pipe is skateboarding at its most rad. When starting out, stick to a half-pipe that's no more than five feet high. Again, begin with a few low and easy kick turns, working your way up the wall gradually. In time you can move on to aerials and other hot moves.

You'll learn a lot of hot stuff just by hanging around half-pipes and watching other skaters. Ask lots of questions. Don't be afraid to let them know that you're learning. Everybody has to learn somehow. Even the champions started at the beginning.

If you hang around good skateboarders, maybe you'll see a really good one do "inverts," or "hand plants." This is when the skateboarder does an aerial, and while he's airborne, flips almost upside down and plants a hand on the coping. For a couple of seconds, he stands on one hand while holding his skateboard to his feet with the other hand.

You probably won't be ready to do this for a long time. You need lots of arm and shoulder strength. Tony Hawk was 12 years old and had been skating three years before he could do a hand plant. "I didn't have the strength to hold myself up," he says. "I couldn't do a handstand to save my life." So don't rush learning hand plants. There are lots of other tricks to master first.

Freestyle Skateboarding

A hot freestyler is sort of like a figure skater. Freestyle skateborders twist and flip their boards in any direction and do any combination of stunts imaginable. Freestylers often do amazingly graceful movements to music. A pro such as Kevin Harris can make his skateboard look alive, almost as if it is jumping and twisting around on its own. But it's really Harris's feet that control the board. A good freestyle skater can walk the board on one edge of the deck, or make the board stand on its tail edge and then stand on the trucks and wheels.

There are dozens of fancy freestyle tricks. Many of them are complicated and require lots of delicate movements. Take it from a pro, Kevin Harris, who believes that freestyle is the hardest style of skating: "You can't just pick it up right away," he advises. "It takes years and years to learn the tricks."

Once you learn a few tricks, freestyle can be the most rewarding form of skating. The best way to learn is to have a friend teach you tricks. You can also learn by watching others. By looking at a trick done over and over, you'll learn some of the finer points eventually. Rent a video of freestyle skating and watch it in slow-motion. You can pause the video wherever you like to analyze a movement step by step. It's almost like having a private teacher in your living room.

A good freestyler can spin, twist and flip a skateboard using just his feet.

CHAPTER 6
PARTS
AND
ACCESSORIES

Owning a skateboard is fun, and it's even more fun to decorate it your own special way. There are lots of cool stickers and decals to put on boards. You can find dozens of them at almost any store that has a large choice of skateboards. Of course, you shouldn't forget a few other items that go with skateboards. These accessories not only make you look good, but they also help you ride better and more safely. You can usually buy them at skateboard shops, too.

One essential item is griptape. This looks like black sandpaper with one sticky side. It helps keep your feet on the board. It's available in either a roll or in pre-cut shapes to fit your board.

Most skaters also like to put rails on the bottom on their boards. Rails are strips of plastic that protect the bottom and give you something to grab when you're doing aerials. They also make the board stronger.

You can also buy plastic nose and tail guards. These help keep the ends of the board from getting splintered and roughed up. Other pieces of plastic protect the trucks. These are called lappers and truck grinders. Lappers go on the rear truck and help guide it over curbs and ramps. However, no matter how many accessories you buy to protect your board, it's still going to take a beating. So let's look at how to take care of your skateboard.

Skateboards don't need a lot of care, but there are a few things to watch. One thing you should do each time before you ride is to make sure the important bolts are tight. These include the bolts that hold the wheels on and the kingpins, which are the bolts that adjust the trucks. The wheel bolts and the kingpins should be snug at all times. About once a month, you should also check the mounting bolts, which hold the base plates of the truck onto the board. These should be tight.

Wheels are probably the first thing that will wear out on your board. After 6 to 12 months of riding, the wheels will start to "cone out," or wear more on the inside than the outside. To prevent this, turn your wheels around about once a month. You have to have reversible wheels to do this. If your wheels aren't reversible—and you'll see that when you remove the bolts and slide the wheels off—then you will have to replace the wheels. Eventually you'll have to replace your wheels whether they're reversible or not. In a year or two, even reversible wheels will be so worn that riding will be uncomfortable and the board will be hard to control.

You'll also have to replace the bearings, which are the metal rollers, or beads, inside the wheels. Like wheels, bearings wear down. Old ones will make a scraping noise, and the wheels will grind and stick, making the board roll unevenly. Replace the wheels and the bearings at the same time. If you turn your wheels regularly, they should last as long as the bearings.

If you ride a board long enough and do enough grinding, eventually you'll wear out the bottom of the trucks. Trucks are made of aluminum, which is a soft metal and wears quickly. It is possible to grind the bottom edge completely away so that you can see the axle inside the truck. When this happens, you may have to replace the truck. One way to prolong the life of your trucks is to buy steel alloy trucks. These are harder and last longer. But they also cost $50 or more.

Naturally, your board isn't the only thing you need to take care of. You should also watch out for yourself. And that means always wearing proper safety equipment when you ride. You can always buy a new board. But you only get one body. Be sure to take care of it as well.

Pads and Helmets

It's important to choose the right kind of pads for the type of skateboarding you are doing. There are two basic kinds of pads: ramp and street. Freestylers usually wear street pads.

Ramp pads are bigger, heavier and protect better than street pads because you usually go faster and fall harder in ramp riding. The plastic disc on a ramp knee pad—called a knee cap—is bigger and stronger than a street pad. There is also more foam padding on the sides and twice as many straps to hold the pad on your leg.

Some ramp knee pads also have extra padding that you can add to the inside. These are called inserts. Some pads also have holes cut into the knee caps. These holes are meant to spread out the shock of a hard fall. One kind works just about as well as the other.

There isn't as much difference between ramp and street elbow pads. The ramp elbow pads are slightly bigger, but you can safely use either kind of elbow pad for either kind of riding.

There are several brands of pads. Rector is the best known because that company has been making pads for about 20 years. Other companies include Dr. Bone Savers, Underground, Aggressor, Scabs and Pro Design.

Choose a helmet with an outer shell of either plastic or fiberglass. The same helmet can be used for street and ramp riding. Many skateboarders prefer plastic helmets even though they cost more. Fiberglass helmets are designed for only one impact. If you fall on your head once, the helmet will be weakened and will not protect your head properly in another fall. If you fall while wearing a fiberglass helmet, you should throw it away and get a new one.

Plastic helmets will usually take several falls before they need replacing. Another advantage of plastic helmets is that they generally come with removable foam liners. These can be replaced with smaller liners so that you don't have to get a bigger helmet if your head grows. Pro-Tec is probably the most common brand of helmet, although there are other good makes, too.

Clothing

Shorts are an important piece of clothing in skateboarding. If you wear the wrong kind, you'll soon know it because they'll be way too tight. Although all your skating clothes should be loose and comfortable, it's especially crucial to wear shorts that give you lots of room to move because you bend at the knees and hips so much. Tight shorts will catch your legs and rear every time you try a rad move. You can buy shorts made just for skateboarding in skateboard shops. They're usually cool looking, with lots of wild patterns.

You can also buy shirts and jackets made especially for skateboarders. Like shorts, they are often baggy and pre-washed to give them a casual look. But you don't have to spend all kinds of money to look like a skater. Any clothes that look totally casual are rad. Lots of skaters make their own clothes out of cut-off jeans, sweat pants or other baggy pants.

The same goes for shirts. Almost all skaters wear t-shirts—preferably oversize ones that are loose and floppy. Just as with shorts, you want shirts that you can move freely in. Lots of skaters like to wear t-shirts with skateboard symbols and logos on them.

The other most important item of clothing is shoes. You'll want something that gives you ankle support. Again, you can buy shoes made especially for skating, and it's not a bad idea to own a pair. Shoes made for skating usually come up over the ankles for extra support. They're also reinforced and trimmed in leather at the toes, heels and ankles, where you tend to wear the shoe out faster. Some of the big names in skating shoes are Vision, Airwalk and Vans. Some skateboard shoes are expensive, but you don't have to spend $60 or more to get a good pair of useful shoes. Lots of skaters wear inexpensive, high-top canvas shoes such as Converse. Like special skateboarding shoes, these come in cool colors.

It's not hard to look cool for skating—just wear anything big, loose and casual. There is no uniform. It's really up to you.

CHAPTER 7

WHERE TO GO SKATE BOARDING

In other areas of the country, though, there are still parks not only with ramps, but also with concrete areas for freestyle and street skating. Some even have curbs, steps and other obstacles just like on the street. And some have big concrete bowls. These look like swimming pools that have been drained. The bowls at parks let you do really rad skating—ollies, aerials and other tricks.

Some parks are indoors and some are outside. When the weather's good, outside parks are more fun. But in winter, indoor parks are usually warmer, drier and more comfortable depending on which part of the country you live in.

Without question, skateboard parks are the best places to go. They have the best ramps and other facilities. Parks are also great for meeting other skaters and learning new tricks. Often, there's a pro or a ''skate patrol'' to help you learn to skate safely.

To find a skateboard park in your city, look in the phone book's yellow pages under ''skateboards.'' If you don't have a park nearby, ask at your skateboard shop where the skaters in your area practice.

Where you skate has a lot of do with what style of skating you like best. If you're a freestyler, you'll probably spend most of your time on sidewalks, at malls and in parking lots. If you're ramp skater, you have to stick to places that have ramps—at skating parks or perhaps in the backyard of a friend who has built his own ramp. Most skaters like to skate a combination of styles. They skate some of the time on ramps and some of the time on pavement.

Skateboard Parks

In some parts of the country, ramps are hard to find. In Southern California many skateboard parks have closed due to troubles with insurance or with communities which do not take to the image of skateboarders, so skaters have had to build their own ramps.

On the Street

Of course, the term ''street skating'' doesn't mean that you should skate in the street. Street are dangerous because drivers of cars often don't see you until it's too late. A lot of kids have been hurt or killed while skateboarding on streets. Don't become one of them.

The best places to do street skating are sidewalks and empty parking lots. Of course, each of these places has its problems. People walk on sidewalks. Give these people lots of room. if anything gives skateboarding a bad name, it's skaters who dodge in and out of pedestrians. Don't do it. Go some place where there's plenty of room and where you can stay away from people on foot.

The problem with parking lots is that they can have just as many cars driving around as the streets do! Be very careful in parking lots. Find one that's almost empty. If there are any cars coming and going, move on. Don't skate anywhere that you see traffic.

It takes years of practice to be good enough to take on a full-pipe. This one is at a skateboard park in southern California.

Swimming Pools

Skateboarding in an empty swimming pool can be a totally cool experience, but it can also cause problems. In some parts of the country, such as California, skaters sneak into private pools when the owners aren't home. Doing something like that may not only get you into trouble with the pool owner, it can also get you arrested by the police. It's called trespassing, and it's illegal. If you skate in a pool, be absolutely sure that you have the owner's permission.

Pool skating gets real gnarly. Hot skaters can ride almost to the top of a pool wall. However, it takes many years of practice to be this good. The best advice is to wait until you've mastered skateboarding before you take on a pool. When you're ready, take a few safety precautions. Find one that's concrete or stone and is oval, round or kidney-shaped and has a steep bottom. Sweep the pool out completely. Cover the lights with cardboard and tape, and cover the drain with a piece of foam or other cushion. And most important, wear your helmet and pads.

Make wide, shallow turns in the pool. You'll find that you have to lean in toward the center of the pool on your turns. And make sure you have a few years of skating on ramps before trying to skate up on the vertical part of the swimming pool wall.

Good Behavior

A lot of people don't like skateboarders. Perhaps they've been hit or even knocked down by skateboarders. Or they have come home and found strangers skateboarding in their driveway or their drained swimming pool.

Even if you're a courteous skater, you're still bound to run into trouble at some time or another. Lots of peo-ple don't understand skateboarders and think they're troublemakers. At least once in your skating career, you will be thrown out of someplace.

Rude skaters ruin it for everybody and give the sport a bad image. Be nice to people. Use good manners, which means being considerate of others. Stay out of the way of people walking and driving, and never skate on private property without asking permission.

One problem with skating at parks is that the ramps often get crowded. When this happens, be careful and stay alert. Skaters run into each other all the time. Show courtesy to other skaters. When others are waiting to drop in, don't hog the ramp. And don't drop in ahead of another skater. This is called "snaking." No one likes people who snake. Let the smaller or less experienced skaters have their turn, too.

Whether you skate at parks, on sidewalks, in parking lots or in drained swimming pools, you may find it tough going from time to time. Parks can get crowded. Sidewalks are often full of pedestrians who don't want you there. Parking lots have traffic. Pools are difficult to skate in and usually off limits. Be sensitive to all these problems and you'll avoid trouble.

The best advice is not to let these things bother you. If you get mad, you'll just make things worse. Be polite and go somewhere else to skate. If all skateboarders start doing that and make sure they skate in the proper places, people will respect them.

A Hot Tip from a Pro

In every other kind of skateboarding, professional skaters agree that the biggest mistake kids make is trying to do tricks that are too advanced for their skills. The result is that too many skaters pick up bad habits. Or they hurt themselves.

"Learn at your own pace," says freestyle superstar Kevin Harris. "Don't try things you're not ready for."

In other words, take it slow and take it easy. With lots of practice, you'll get wired and have a lot of fun!

SNOWBOARDING

FINDING THE RIGHT SNOWBOARD

The half-pipe gets its name because from the side it looks like half a pipe.

Alpine snowboarding, on the other hand, is all other forms of snowboarding down a mountain. In alpine, you take a chairlift to the top of the mountain and then slide down, cutting back and forth across the slope. Alpine snowboarding also includes competitive events such as slalom racing, in which you go as fast as you can on a course marked by gates, or poles stuck in the snow.

The decision is yours. Do you like hotdogging? Jumping? Twisting, turning and getting lots of air? If so, then you're a freestyler. If you prefer carving long, graceful turns and going fast, then you're more of an alpine rider.

I f you're thinking of buying a snowboard right away, here's some advice: Don't do it. A big difference between snowboards and the two other kinds of rad boards is cost. Good snowboards cost $200 to $400, while bodyboards range from $50 to $125, and skateboards can go for as little as $25 to $150 for a custom model. You don't want to spend that much money until you've been snowboarding a few times. Then you'll know whether you like the sport, and you will know what kind of board to buy.

Snowboarding Styles

Before you buy a snowboard, you must first decide which of the two styles of snowboarding you will be doing: freestyle or alpine. In freestyle, you do tricks and aerials on the slopes and in half-pipes, which are downhill chutes with snow-covered walls facing each other.

To Rent or to Buy: That's the Question!

You'll only know which style appeals to you after you have gone snowboarding a few times and learned the basics. Rent a board the first few times you go. After you learn to turn, to stop, and to control the board, you can experiment with different sizes of boards, and you can even try a few tricks.

One suggestion for beginners is to buy an all-around alpine board. These boards are in the same price-range as other snowboards, but they're the most versatile and you can use them to slide down the mountain or to perform a few freestyle moves. It's also a great board to learn on because you will probably fall a lot. Because the board is not as elaborate as a super fancy one, you won't mind as much if it gets banged up. By the time you are ready for a new board, you will know what kind of board you want, and you won't be falling as often.

Demos

You should also ask a local ski store if it is possible to rent or borrow a ''demo.'' Demo is short for demonstration model. Many stores rent them for $15 to $30 a day. Renting different demo boards on several different days is a great way to test ride several different boards. This will help you choose the board that's right for you. Many shops will let you deduct any rent you've paid from the price of a board if you buy one from that shop.

A good entry-level board will have several features. First, the tip and tail will be turned up at the ends. That way, the edges won't dig into the snow when you go forward or do a fakie—which means going backwards.

Second, the board shouldn't have too much ''sidecut,'' which is important when you turn because it allows the entire edge of the board to stay in contact with the snow. If there's too much sidecut, the board turns too easily and it becomes unstable for a beginning rider.

An entry-level board should also have soft flex. Snowboards are made to bend as you jump, go over bumps and turn. Stiff boards are faster, but they are harder to control. A soft-flex board makes learning the basic moves easier.

Generally, it's hard to go wrong by picking a name-brand board designed for beginners. The three best-known brands of snowboards are Burton, Sims and Kemper. Snowboarding's a fast growing sport, and traditional alpine ski companies, such as Rossignol, are now producing complete lines of snowboards and equipment. There are currently at least two dozen other brands, and many have excellent boards for beginners.

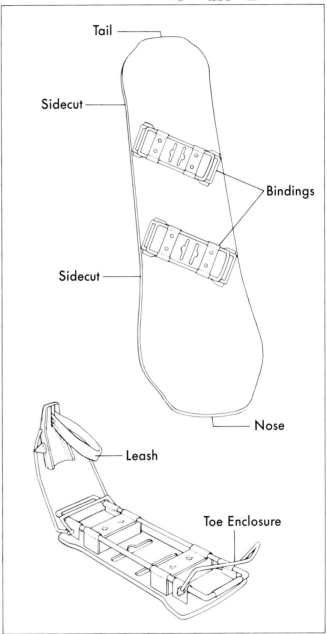

Tail

Sidecut

Bindings

Sidecut

Nose

Leash

Toe Enclosure

A typical snowboard, and bindings to hold your feet on the board. A beginner should choose a soft flex board—one that bends a little to make learning basic moves easier.

What to Avoid

There are a few cheapies on the market to stay away from. Any new board that costs less than about $200 may be unsafe. Boards that sell for far less then $100 often have plastic bindings that break easily and can cause serious injury. Good snowboards are expensive because they are hard to make. It takes fancy equipment and technology to glue and bend strips of wood for the core and then cover it in layers of plastic. But the expense pays off. A good board doesn't lose its flex, it is far more stable and turns easily. Most important, a well-made board is a safe board.

Board Sizes

After you've selected a particular model and brand, you need to decide what size of snowboard to buy. Snowboards are measured in centimeters. A centimeter is a little less than a half inch. Generally, snowboards for beginners come in three lengths: 135 to 140 centimeters for people who weigh 135 pounds or less; 150 centimeters for people who weigh from 136 to 150 pounds; and 165 centimeters for people who weigh more than 150 pounds. Your height is also a factor. If you're really tall, you may want to move up to a board that is one size larger than is indicated by your weight. If you stand a board on its tail, its tip should be four to five inches below your chin.

Where To Buy

When you're ready to buy, find a shop that specializes in snowboards and ask a salesperson to help you make your final choice. You can find these stores near ski areas or in large cities. Many of these shops also sell skis and outdoor clothing. That's usually a sign that the people who work at the shop are dedicated to snow sports.

Be careful about buying a board from a department store or a discount sporting goods store. These stores may sell snowboards only as a sideline and may not have knowledgeable salesmen. Stick to the specialty stores.

CHAPTER 9

GETTING STARTED

The Importance of Lessons

Lessons are a good idea for beginners. You learn much faster from a trained snowboarding instructor. Most ski areas offer classes for beginners, and some offer free lessons. Lessons will probably include the free rental of a snowboard.

At some ski areas, you must be certified before you can ride the chairlift. This means that you must demonstrate that you can get on and off the lift safely, and that you know how to stop when you're snowboarding downhill. Once you're certified, you usually get a card to keep in a pocket or wear around your neck.

If you don't know how to snowboard, you can't get certified to ride the lifts. And if you can't ride the lifts, you can't learn how to snowboard. Most people can learn enough to be certified after just a few lessons. Before you hit the slopes, though, you'd better make sure you're dressed properly. Wintertime is cold in the mountains, and you'll probably fall down a lot at first. You'll have more fun and be able to concentrate better if you're not shivering, so dress warmly.

About the worst thing you can wear are blue jeans and other cotton clothes. Cotton gets wet quickly and it dries slowly. Instead, try to find ski pants, a ski jump suit or other nylon clothes that will repel water. The same goes for gloves. Knitted gloves will just soak up water from the snow. Instead, wear leather or nylon ski or snowboarding gloves.

Basic Moves

Strapping In

The first thing to learn is how to attach the board to your feet. If you're right-handed, you probably have rented a board with the bindings set up so your left foot is the front foot. (The bindings are those plastic pieces on top of the board that hold your foot to the board.) This means you're a "regular footed" rider. If you try

By far, the best place to go snowboarding is at a ski slope, especially now that most ski areas welcome snowboarders. Ski areas are great because they provide chair lifts to take you to the top of the hill that you plan to ride down. You can walk up, of course, but walking takes so much energy and time that it's not really worth it. You'll have much more fun letting a chairlift do all the work.

Another reason for going to a ski resort is that the slopes are almost always groomed. That means that the snow is smoothed over by special tractors called Snow Cats. On a groomed slope, most of the ruts, hidden holes and other rough areas will have been covered with snow. Ski resorts are also safer. Ski patrols monitor the slopes to help injured people and to make sure everyone obeys the rules. They also open and close trails depending on snow conditions. Unstable snow can cause avalanches, which sometimes kill people. For this reason, you should never snowboard outside the boundaries of a ski area.

This downhill racer is shifting his weight to the right and turning his snowboard onto its edge as he gets ready to turn in that direction.

riding regular footed and it doesn't feel right, then it may be that you're "goofy-footed,"—which means that your right foot should be the forward foot.

Don't let the term "goofy-footed" stop you from turning around and putting your right foot in front. More than a third of all snowboarders ride that way, including world champion Andy Hetzel. Either way you ride, the forward foot is the only one you'll strap to the board to start with. You have to keep the rear foot free to get to the chairlift.

If it's really cold or windy outside, you'll also need an insulated jacket. Again, a ski jacket is best. Otherwise, wear a sweater and a t-shirt or a windbreaker over a long-sleeved shirt. A lot of people also wear long underwear beneath their pants and jackets for extra warmth. Long underwear is a good idea on any day that the temperature is below 25°F.

Top off your outfit with a hat and a pair of goggles or sunglasses. A knitted ski cap will keep you almost

twice as warm as wearing nothing at all. As for eyewear, your goggles or sunglasses should be tinted to protect against glare and ultraviolet rays of the sun. Look for a sticker on the glasses or goggles that says the lenses have UV (ultraviolet) protection. If you wear sunglasses, use a tight strap to keep them from falling off and stabbing you with the earpieces if you take a headfirst fall.

Finally, the last thing you need to put on is sunscreen. Even on a cloudy day, you can get a bad sunburn at a ski resort. Sunlight is stronger up in the mountains because there is less atmosphere to block the sun's rays. Snow also reflects sunlight. So use lots of sunscreen on your face, especially your nose, which can get burned first.

Now, you're finally ready to face the mountain!

Close the plastic buckles of the front binding around your forward boot. Always buckle the middle strap first. Also wrap the safety strap around your leg and buckle it. The safety strap will keep the snowboard from sliding away and hitting someone if you fall and your foot pops out of the bindings.

Now that you're strapped in, stand up and practice the basic snowboarding position: Stand with your back straight, your knees bent and your body loose. This stance will help you absorb bumps on the hill and give you better control in turns.

Now use your rear foot (only your front foot should be buckled to the board) to push yourself around on the snow. To do this, push yourself along as you would on a skateboard. You might find it easier if you rock the heel of your forward foot so that the board rides on one edge. Get used to putting the board on edge like this. That's how you ride most of the time.

Falling

One thing you should get used to is falling. Snowboarders call this "biffing." There is no way to learn snowboarding without taking tumbles. All snowboarders fall down—even Craig Kelly, who is considered the best freestyler in the world. "If I'm trying new tricks and pushing myself," Kelly says, "I'll definitely fall. Of course, if it's a day when conditions are icy, I go out of my way not to fall. I try to save the hard tricks for a slushy day or powdery day."

You never know when you're going to fall. In 1990, Chris Karol, a former national and world champion and one of the world's fastest snowboarders, fell on a race course while he was going 75 miles per hour. Karol slid on his back for at least 50 feet, and then he jumped to his feet and continued snowboarding. He wasn't hurt because he knew how to fall properly.

Before you get on the chairlift, practice falling safely. A "bunny slope" or a flat, open area is the perfect place to practice. To practice falling, stand with the board positioned sideways across the hill. This is the position the board should be in when you stop. Otherwise, gravity will pull you and the board down the hill. The most direct route down the hill is called the "fall line." Whenever you're stopped, keep the board at right angles to the fall line.

Next, strap your rear foot into the binding and practice getting your body into position. Bend your knees and waist slightly and turn your head to look ahead

With her front foot strapped in, a snowboarder is ready to head for the ski lift.

and over your forward shoulder. Lean slightly up the hill. Raise your arms to about waist level and bend your elbows slightly. This is a lot like the basic skateboard position. Now, take a few tumbles from this position. The key is to fall on your knees and forearms, not your hands. The most important rule in falling is DON'T USE YOUR HANDS. You may end up spraining or breaking your arms, wrists or fingers. These are the most common injuries in snowboarding. If you find yourself falling forward, bend at the knees, elbows and waist, close your fists and try to let yourself land gently on your elbows and knees.

In a backward fall, just as in a forward fall, bend your knees, elbows and waist and try to land on your arms instead of your hands. If it's a particularly hard fall, try rolling to one side or the other as you hit the snow. This helps spread the shock across your body.

The Side-Slip

Backward

Now, you're ready to learn how to side-slip, or snowplow. The side-slip is used for braking and stopping. You can do it either forward or backward, though a backward side-slip is easier for most people.

To do a backward side-slip turn so that the board is across the fall line and you are facing uphill. You may have to unbuckle your rear foot temporarily to turn the board. Bend your knees and flex your ankles to roll the board up onto its uphill edge. This will stop the board from sliding sideways down the hill. Next, slowly tilt the board back down so it is flat on the snow. You'll notice that the board starts to slide sideways downhill. To stop, tilt the board onto its uphill edge again. This is called a backward side-slip because you are facing backward while the board slides sideways downhill.

Practice starting and stopping. Don't be discouraged if the board starts to turn downhill—you can always stop by falling correctly. Turn the board back across the hill, stand up and try again. You'll get it right real soon.

Forward

The forward side-slip, or snowplow, is just like the backward side-slip except that you face downhill instead of uphill. The forward side-slip is a little harder to do, but it lets you see where you're going. You'll appreciate this move if you accidentally end up on a steep slope. Another place that it comes in handy is on a slope that has lots of big bumps in the snow. These are called "moguls."

Moguls are caused by skiers turning time after time in the same places on the hill. Snowboarding through them is called "shredding the bumps." It's fun, but very difficult. Sometimes you'll want to just side-slip through them.

To do a forward side-slip, start with a heel turn. (Read about heel turns in the section on Turning in Chapter 10.) Before finishing the turn, shift some of your weight back to the rear foot. Keep your board across the hill and slide downhill by rolling your toes forward to make the snowboard lie flat on the snow. To slow down or stop, rock your heels backward to dig the uphill edge of the board into the snow. You'll find that you can completely control your speed by rolling your ankles slightly.

Once you've mastered side-slipping and turning, you should be able to get down most slopes. You may not always get down gracefully, but if you take it slow and easy—side-slipping all the way if necessary—you will get down, that's a promise!

You'll be smart, though, if you stick to the beginning and intermediate slopes for awhile. You'll learn faster there and have more fun. It can be frustrating for you and dangerous to skiers and other snowboarders if you are on a slope that's too steep or full of moguls.

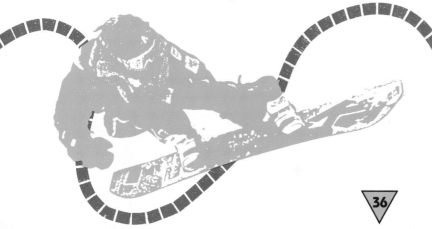

If this snowboarder had learned how to brake by using a forward side-slip, maybe he wouldn't be heading over a cliff! Actually, he will land on snow just a few feet below and keep going.

The Chairlift

Getting On

Now it's time to ride the chairlift up the mountain. Getting on the lift is a bit tricky. It involves careful timing.

Take your rear foot out of its binding so that you can push yourself to the loading area. You have to wait in line with the other skiers until it's your turn and the lift attendant gives you the okay to board. As soon as the people ahead of you get into their chair, scoot into the path of the oncoming chair.

There will probably be a wooden or plastic marker across the snow to show you where to stop and wait for the chair. Stand at the marker and point your board straight ahead. Look back over your shoulder so you can see the chair coming. When it gets to you, grab the chair back or side rail, bend your knees, and sit. Lift the nose of your snowboard and keep it up until you're out of the boarding area. You can rest the board on your free foot or, if there is one, on the foot-rest bar that swings down from overhead.

You made it! You're on your way uphill.

Getting Off

Getting off the lift is like the reverse of getting on. When your chair gets close to the end, lift the nose of your board and guide it down to the snow. Grab the edge of the seat with your right hand (left for goofy-footers) to steady yourself. Then stand up with your rear foot on the board just ahead of the back binding. You'll naturally slide forward out of the way of the chair.

If you fall, get up as fast as you can. Or at least crawl out of the way of the people getting off the lift behind you. You don't want to be run over, or be the cause of a 10-person pile-up. It's definitely not cool to snowboard with ski tracks across your back.

Now comes the big moment. You're ready to try real snowboarding. Your first few runs may be frustrating. You won't feel as if you have much control over the board. Keep trying, though. If you follow the instructions in the next chapter, you'll find yourself learning quickly.

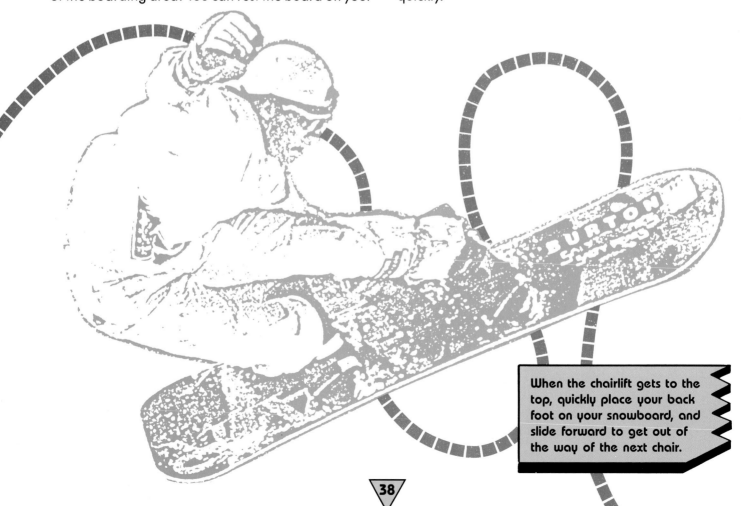

When the chairlift gets to the top, quickly place your back foot on your snowboard, and slide forward to get out of the way of the next chair.

After you've gotten off the lift safely at the top of the hill, you're ready to learn how to turn. Push yourself to an uncrowded area, and then place your board across the fall line and buckle your back binding. First practice the basic snowboarding position. Stay loose and keep your back straight and your knees bent. This stance will give you better control in turns.

Weighting and Unweighting

To learn how to turn on a snowboard, you'll need to get used to getting up a little speed and shifting your weight from one foot to the other. Start out with a side-slip to get yourself moving. The board may want to turn and start to go downhill, almost as if it has a mind of its own. That's okay. Let it go.

When you put weight on your front foot, the nose of the board turns downhill. When you put weight evenly on both feet, the board turns sideways on the hill. This is how every snowboarder controls the board's direction.

As you shift your weight to your front foot, the board will turn downhill. Suddenly you will begin picking up speed. Don't panic. Make sure to keep your knees bent and your weight forward. As you pick up speed, you'll probably want to bend at the waist and lean back. Most beginners fight speed by leaning in the opposite direction of the downhill pull of gravity. That's wrong. Fight the urge. Remember, you control the board by keeping your hips and weight forward over your front foot.

Toe Turns

Obviously, there are two directions you can turn: left or right. One is called a "toe turn," and the other is a "heel turn." Try a toe turn first. It's called a toe turn because you lean the board up on the edge that's closest to your toes. If you're a regular rider, with your left foot forward, this will be a turn to the right. If you're a goofy-footer, which means you ride with your right foot forward, a toe turn is to the left.

To start a turn, bend at the knees and drive your hips forward over your front foot as though you're about to dance "the bump" with someone. At the same time, shift most of your weight to your front foot. Then, with elbows bent, point both hands downhill. By pointing your hands and keeping your weight forward, your body will lead the board into the turn.

Finish the turn by pushing the tail of the board down the hill with your rear foot. It helps to think of your rear foot as your kicking foot: It kicks the tail of the board through the rest of the turn. The front foot acts as a pivot, and the rear foot always rotates around the front foot.

The trick is to do everything in one smooth motion. It's also important to keep your weight forward and to not let either hand touch the snow. Chris Karol, who runs a snowboarding camp every summer in Oregon, is one of the best snowboarding teachers around. He tells beginning snowboarders not to "pat the dog." He means you should not drag your palm across the snow as though you're reaching down and patting a dog.

Karol's rule is so important that he named an instructional video "Don't Pat the Dog." Once you've learned the basics, watching Karol's video is an excellent way to improve your turns. You can order the video by writing to the address given in the Appendix at the end of this book.

Linking Turns
1. To link a heel turn with a toe turn, start by unweighting—lifting your weight off the board—by springing up with your knees or doing a little hop.

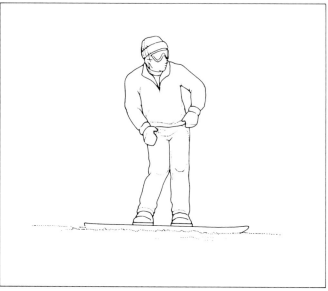

2. Before moving into a toe turn, make sure most of your weight is over your front foot. This gives you control over your snowboard. Now lean your weight toward your toes so that your snowboard tilts onto the toe edge.

3. You will turn in an arc in the direction your feet are pointing. After you've started turning, slide your tail out by using your rear leg to push it downhill. This will slow you down a little. Then unweight again, and go into a heel turn.

Heel Turns

As you practice toe turns, you'll quickly realize that a toe turn only allows you to turn one way, and when you get to the other side of the slope, you have to stop. There are two ways to get back to the other side: You can either sit down and flip the board around so that it's headed the other way, or you can do a heel turn.

A heel turn is a turn on the edge of the board that's closest to your heels. For regular-foot riders, a heel turn is to the left, the opposite of a toe turn. For goofy-footers, a heel turn goes right.

To make a heel turn, again start by driving your hips forward and weighting your front foot. Point your hands in the direction you want to turn. You'll find that your body and the board tend to follow your shoulders, arms and hands in whatever direction you steer them. Again, push the tail of the board through the turn with your rear foot.

You'll find it easier to turn in one direction than the other. This is natural. Work on your weaker turn by practicing it more. You'll probably also fall a lot on both heel and toe turns. Don't worry. Falling is natural. Just remember to fall safely: Bend your knees and elbows and drop gently onto your forearms.

Once you start to turn smoothly, you can take on steeper slopes. All you have to do is zigzag down the hill, using the toe turns on one side of the slope and heel turns on the other side. This is called "traversing." Skiers traverse steep slopes, too. There may even be skiers traversing the slope you are on, so watch out so that you don't collide with one.

Linking Turns

As you get better at turning, you can start connecting heel and toe turns together. This is where you really look cool. Good snowboarders can turn left and right so fast that they look as though their board is attached to a track in the snow.

To link turns together quickly, you have to learn what is called a weight transfer. This means that from turn to turn you shift your weight from one edge of the snowboard to the other. In between, you will actually be weightless for a fraction of a second. During that moment, your board will run flat across the snow, or it may even be airborne an inch or two above the snow.

Many snowboarders learn how to make smooth weight transfers by hopping from turn to turn. For example, as you're coming out of a toe turn, spring upward and forward. Swing your legs under you and push the board forward so that it lands on the heel edge. You have just hopped from a toe turn into a heel turn.

On wide turns, bend your knees and waist more and drop a little lower. On a wide toe turn, drive your shoulders and knees farther forward. On a wide heel turn, drop your rear as if you're about to sit in the snow. On tight turns, keep your upper body higher. Let your knees do most of the work, and don't raise your arms and hands quite as much.

Practice linking your turns. Soon you will be able to turn almost as fast as the pros. Then you'll be just as rad as they are.

Another important turn to learn is the carved turn. This may even be the most important move in snowboarding. To carve a turn, you put the board up on an edge and let your weight bend the board into an arc through the turn. This arc gives you far better speed and control than if you simply skid the board through turns. A carving turn is the turn that pros use to win speed races and to do the fanciest tricks.

Carved turns are especially crucial in the half-pipe. (You can read more about the half-pipe in the next section.) "If you don't carve in the half-pipe," says Craig Kelly, "any bumps will tend to knock you over."

Principles of Carving

The "side cut" of a snowboard is what allows you to carve. If you lay a board on its side, you'll notice that the edge near the tip and tail touches the ground, while the edge in the middle of the board is an inch or so off the ground.

When you stand on the board and lean on one edge, your body weight will bend the board so that the edge stays in contact with the ground. Your entire snowboard bends into an arc, and this arc is what carves the turn across the snow. One thing you can do to help the board carve is to weight the board forcefully on each turn. As you finish a weight transfer from one turn to another, bend you knees and then press down hard. And stay low—it helps your balance.

"As soon as I start getting out of balance," says Chris Karol, "I dip my weight low. It's a sure-fire recovery."

This goofy-footed snow-boarder is carving a toe turn to the left. She keeps her hands forward to help balance her body, and control her turns.

Hands

Your hands also play an important role in helping you carve turns. Remember reading earlier about pointing your hands in the direction of your turn? As you improve your skills, you can relax that motion a bit. Instead, keep your hands in front of you, and keep them pointed downhill.

Craig Kelly says he imagines that his hands are on a steering wheel guiding him down the mountain. This keeps his hands forward and over the board. His shoulders and hands are pointed down the hill, and they don't move very much. His lower body, from the waist down, is about the only part of him that moves as he carves turns.

Keeping your hands forward also helps to keep you from leaning backward as your board picks up speed. As we mentioned earlier, many beginners have a bad habit of leaning back. Keeping your hands forward also balances your lower body when you bend at the knees and hips to angle the board into a carved turn. If you don't keep your hands forward, you might end up sitting in the snow on a heel turn or collapsing to your knees during a toe turn. This doesn't look too cool.

On long, fast heel turns, you should force your rear hand forward. Chris Karol drops his hips so low that he's almost sitting in the snow. Then he reaches forward with his rear hand as if he's going to grab the front edge of the snowboard. This is called counterbalancing. By reaching forward with his hand, it helps him keep his weight over his board even though his hips are behind the board.

You should also counterbalance on a long, fast toe turn. The only difference is that you reach forward with your forward hand instead of your rear hand. If you use your hands properly, you'll find that the rest of your body moves into place naturally.

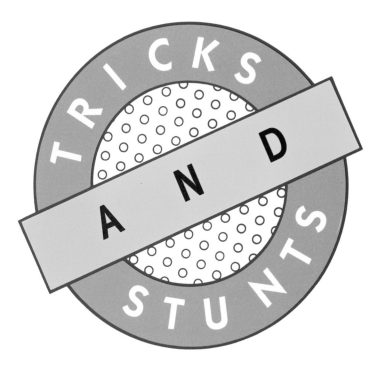

CHAPTER 11

If you spend time around snowboarders, you'll see fancy tricks with cool names like ''the stalefish,'' ''the roastbeef'' and ''the slob.'' Sooner or later, you'll want to try these tricks yourself. This style of snowboarding is called ''freestyle.'' But before you attempt any freestyle tricks, you need to find a safe place to practice.

First, find out the rules at your favorite ski area. Some ski areas allow stunts only in half-pipes—those long chutes with banks of snow on both sides. It's called a half-pipe, of course, because it looks like a big snow pipe that has its top half cut off. These are like skateboarding half-pipes, and many snowboard tricks are similar to skateboard tricks. Half-pipes are only for advanced snowboarders. You'll need lots of practice before you can take on a half-pipe.

The best way to learn simple tricks is to build a snow ramp 12 to 18 inches high. A ski area may allow you to do this in an uncrowded area off the major slopes. Ask the ski patrol first. You can also look for a small bump to the side of a ski trail. Or you can build your own snow ramp in your backyard or in a public park. Build your ramp on a slight slope, and be sure that the landing area is also sloped downhill. You don't want to land on flat ground—you'll land too hard.

Aerials

The first trick to learn is simply ''catching air'' or an ''aerial.'' Ride slowly down the hill and up the ramp. Just as you reach the edge, bend your knees and hop the board off the lip. As you land, bend your knees to absorb the shock.

Craig Kelly believes that landing is the most important part of getting air. A smooth landing makes the rest of the maneuver look smooth. Practice easy jumps over and over. As you gain confidence, you can try jumping a little higher. Eventually you'll get enough air to try tricks while you're airborne.

Basic Tricks

The fundamental tricks all involve bending at the knees, and reaching down and grabbing the board with one hand while you're airborne. For example, to do a ''method,'' grab the heel edge of the board near the nose with your forward hand (the left hand for regular footers; the right hand for goofy-footers). To do a ''mute,'' grab the toe edge of the board near the nose.

As you get more comfortable doing aerials, methods and mutes, you can move to a half-pipe. Of course, not every ski area has a half-pipe. You may have to look hard for one that does.

A snowboarder does an awesome handplant on the lip of a half-pipe.

Half-Pipe Stunts

It helps to know the basic parts of a half-pipe. The bottom is called the "flat." The lower part of the wall is called the "transition." The top is the "vert," meaning that the wall is actually straight up and down for a foot or two. The top edge is called the "lip," and the flat area on top is known as the "roll-out." Not all half-pipes have true "vert." You should start on a smaller half-pipe that doesn't have vert—one with walls no more than about four feet high. Save the big 10-foot walls with vert for later.

Dropping In

A good place to start in a half-pipe is at the upper end, where there's usually a short ramp for easy stunts. The ramp may be only one or two feet high. That's enough to get you plenty of air for now.

On your first few runs, start about 10 feet up the ramp from where you'll drop over the edge into the half-pipe. Make sure no one is in your way. Wait until the snowboarder ahead of you has made at least two turns off the walls of the half-pipe. Let other snowboarders know that you're about to start by calling out, "Dropping in!" As in skateboarding and bodyboarding, "dropping in" means that you're dropping into the half-pipe or wave.

At first, just do simple aerials off the ramp and don't worry about trying to grab or turn the board. Next, try making turns off the walls of the half-pipe, and then do a turn followed by an aerial.

Riding the Walls

For your first few times in a half-pipe, work on making easy, gradual turns on both walls. Don't go very far up the wall, and carve your turns. Carved turns will help you get through the ruts and tracks left in the snow by other snowboarders.

The walls of the half-pipe are called a "front-side" wall and a "back-side" wall. You do heel turns on the front-side wall. This is the right wall for regular-footers and the left wall for goofy-footers. You do toe turns off the back-side wall. Sooner or later, you'll graduate to getting air off both walls. Then you'll actually be turning partly in the air instead of completely on snow. As you get comfortable getting air, you can start adding basic moves such as the method and the mute that you learned on the ramp.

You should do both the method air and the mute air on the backside wall. To do a method air, you simply grab the board near the nose with your front hand on the heel edge. As you might guess, a mute air is when you do the same thing on the toe edge.

Cool Moves

You'll probably find it easier to get a little fancier on the front-side wall. Most snowboarders do. For example, you can do a "stalefish" by reaching behind you and grabbing the heel edge between your bindings. To do a "roastbeef," you reach between your legs and grab the heel edge between the bindings.

Another cool front-side trick is the "slob." To do this, you grab the toe edge near the nose with your front hand and "bone out" your rear leg for a moment. This means that you make your leg a little straighter, momentarily twisting the tail of the board around so that, for a fraction of a second, the board is at a right angle to the direction of the half-pipe.

There are dozens of variations on these simple moves. To "tweak" the board, you hold the bone out position a little longer. A "crail" is the same as a slob except that you use the back hand to grab the toe edge.

Some snowboard tricks are the same in skateboarding. A "rock 'n' roll" in skateboarding, for example, is when you momentarily straddle the board on the coping (the top edge) of one side of a half-pipe. In snowboarding, the rock 'n' roll is practically the same—the only difference is that you slip-slide along the lip at the edge of a half-pipe.

Advanced Tricks

Just as in skateboarding, there are so many snow-boarding tricks that no one knows them all, not even Craig Kelly, who practices snowboarding 200 days a year. New tricks are being invented all the time. Still, you can learn lots of tricks by hanging out with and watching other snowboarders. The stunts covered here will give you plenty of basics to build other tricks on.

With time, you may even see expert snowboarders do such fancy stunts as hand plants and 360s. A hand plant is where you do a hand stand on the lip of a half-pipe. A 360 is a full turn off the vert of a half-pipe. Both are truly awesome tricks to watch, but be careful about trying these yourself. You can seriously hurt your head, neck or joints if you fall the wrong way. Wait until you've had lots of practice with other basic tricks first. You'll have plenty of other flashy stuff to work on in the meantime.

PARTS AND ACCESSORIES

As you get better on the snowboard, you'll want to own your own equipment. The first piece you buy will probably be the board itself. At the same time, you'll pick out bindings and a pair of boots. Then you may also want to think about getting snowboarding clothes. These not only look hot, but they also have special features that are very practical. First, let's look at the equipment that goes on your feet.

Boots and Bindings

Bindings are included in the purchase price of a ready-made board. However, you have a choice of two basic kinds. Most snowboarders use freestyle bindings. These are made of plastic and come up the back of your calf, or lower leg. They give you lots of support but are more flexible than plate bindings. Plate bindings look like ski bindings. A metal or plastic plate is attached to the board, and wire fasteners attach the plate to the toes and heels of specially-made boots.

Don't buy plate bindings if you're a beginner. Plate bindings are made to go with hard plastic boots. They make your feet and ankles much more rigid than freestyle bindings and boots. They are mostly for high-speed alpine riding, and they cost about twice as much as freestyle bindings. Freestyle bindings and soft boots are far more versatile, and soft boots are a lot more comfortable to walk around in.

You also have a choice of two-buckle or three-buckle freestyle bindings. The three-buckle system is identical to a two-buckle binding except that it has a nylon strap with a plastic buckle that goes around the shin. Three buckles give you more support, so a three-buckle binding is a better choice for all-around riding. But a two-buckle system is better if you plan to stay in the half-pipe.

As for footwear, several snowboard companies make soft boots to go with freestyle bindings. These are a lot like ordinary felt-lined snow boots except that they have plastic-bladder linings instead of felt. If you already have a pair of felt-lined boots, you can wear them as they are, or you can convert them to snowboarding boots. You can do this by going to garage sales and finding an old pair of ski boots with removeable bladders. Then simply replace the felt lining in your boots with the ski-boot bladder. The bladder will make the boot stiffer and give you more control over your board. In the meantime, you've saved the cost of new snow-boarding boots.

One final piece of equipment you may need is a leash. This is the nylon strap that is attached to your board and to your leg. Leashes are supposed to keep your board from running away from you and hitting someone if your feet pop out of your bindings. That almost never happens, but many ski areas don't let you on the chairlift without a leash. So it's a good idea to have one. If nothing else, leashes are useful for wrapping around your wrist when you carry a board across a slope. That way, if you fall and let go of your board, it won't go careening into someone else—or sailing downhill while you're standing at the top! So go ahead and spring for one. It shouldn't cost more than $10, and it may make a lot of chairlift attendants happy.

Clothing and Accessories

When you're learning to snowboard, it's easy to rent boards and boots. But you have to supply your own clothes. Chances are that you don't already have all the perfect snowboarding clothes, so you'll probably have to fake it for a while. Like skateboarding clothes, snowboard apparel needs to fit loosely. You're going to spend a lot of time out in the wind and falling in the snow, so your clothing also should be water- and wind-resistant. Ski clothes are usually designed for this, but they can also fit a little too tightly for snowboarding. If you already have ski clothes, though, go ahead and wear them. Later on, if you get serious about snowboarding, you can buy a special outfit.

Snowboarding clothes are designed to look and feel good. The elbows of jackets and the knees and seats of pants are usually reinforced with extra layers of fabric. After all, those are the parts of your body that you land on most often when you fall.

Some jackets and pants are insulated with a special filling designed to help keep the warmth inside. Jackets may also have a high collar to block the wind, and an elastic or drawstring waist to keep out snow. Pants may have an extra layer of fabric in the ankle area, along with an elastic cuff, to help keep out snow.

Snowboard gloves are some of the best made sporting goods available. They are usually filled with a high-tech insulation to keep your hands warm. The fingers are coated in a flexible plastic to protect against wear when you are doing tricks and grabbing the edges of your board. The outside is coated with a special water-proof material to keep your hands dry. Some gloves even have heavy padding on the outside to protect your hands when you slam a gate out of the way in an alpine slalom competition.

The big drawback to buying special gloves and clothes for snowboarding is price. It's not hard to spend $500 on a complete outfit. Gloves alone may cost nearly $100. It will probably take you several birthdays and Christmases to acquire a complete snowboarding outfit. Be patient. It's good to find out first if you're going to be serious enough about the sport to make these purchases worthwhile.

Two other accessories that come in handy are snowboard bags and carrying straps. Bags are nice to have if you fly or ride a bus and have to check your equipment as baggage. Snowboard bags are usually made of heavy nylon that will protect the board and bindings from getting nicked and scratched. Some are even roomy enough to hold your boots.

Snowboard straps are handy if you do a lot of walking up mountains or half-pipes. They attach to the bindings and come with a padded shoulder strap that makes the board much more comfortable to carry. By now you've probably noticed that there's lots to buy for snowboarding and that it's not a cheap sport. It's easy to spend $1,000 to fully outfit yourself with a board, boots and clothes. Of course, you can always get by spending far less. One way to save money is to buy used equipment. Look for second-hand gear at garage sales and ski swaps. Or advertise for used equipment in a local newspaper.

Another way to save money is to not buy the most expensive stuff. You won't need top-of-the-line gear for a long time. And clothing made by snowboard companies often costs more than water- and wind-resistant clothes made for some other sports. Shop around. It will pay off.

Meanwhile, start filling out your Christmas and birthday wish lists, and consider mowing lawns or delivering newspapers to earn extra money. If you're truly interested in being a snowboarder, you'll eventually find a way to get what you need.

As you read earlier, ski areas are really the only places to go snowboarding. They are by far the safest and the most fun. The slopes are groomed, and there are ski patrols to help you. Ski areas are also a great place to meet other snowboarders.

Half-Pipes

Ski areas are also where you'll find half-pipes. Unlike skateboard half-pipes, snowboard half-pipes take a lot of money and special earth- and snow-moving equipment to build. Some are made out of dirt and covered with snow. Others are constructed completely from snow. It's not unusual for a half-pipe to cost $30,000 to build. At that price, you obviously can't afford to build one in your backyard.

A number of ski areas are famous among snowboarders for having good half-pipes. Two ski areas that are favorites of snowboarders are at Stratton Mountain in Vermont and Breckenridge in Colorado.

Stratton Mountain usually hosts the national championships, and Breckenridge holds world cup races. You'll see lots of snowboarders at both these resorts. Of course, other resorts have half-pipes, even small ones in places such as Pennsylvania and Ohio. As snowboarding gets more popular, resort operators are realizing the importance of building half-pipes for board riders.

Any resort that's popular for its half-pipe can get crowded. Whenever you're in a half-pipe, you should use proper etiquette, just as skateboarders do in their half-pipes. Don't "snake" anybody, or drop in ahead of another boarder who was waiting ahead of you. When starting from a ramp at the top of a half-pipe, let the snowboarder before you make at least two turns off the walls before you start.

At some ski areas, it's easier to walk up to the half-pipe than it is to take the chairlift. The nearest chairlift may be too far away to make it worthwhile. The ski area may require that you buy a lift ticket anyway, regardless of whether you ride the lifts. If that happens, be a good sport and don't complain. Remember, ski areas use money they make from selling lift tickets to pay for grooming the slopes, building half-pipes and putting the ski patrol out on the mountain. It's only fair that you pay your way.

Safety First

Snowboarding can be a very dangerous sport, so safety is crucial. One place that you definitely do not want to snowboard is in the woods. Some videos show expert snowboarders ripping through forests, but you should *absolutely* stay away from them. It's very dangerous. Hit a tree hard and you'll end up in the hospital, or maybe even dead.

No matter where you practice, be courteous of skiers and other snowboarders. Among many skiers, snowboarders have the bad image of being rude and reckless. It's important to change that. Give skiers and other snowboarders plenty of respect and show people that snowboarders can courteously share the hill with everyone else.

BODYBOARDING

CHAPTER 14

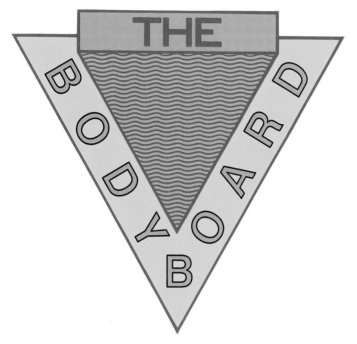

THE BODY BOARD

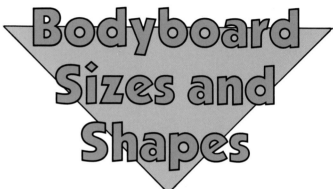

Bodyboard Sizes and Shapes

Boards to Avoid

G enerally, a bodyboard is defined as a short, soft and flexible surfboard. Surfboards and bellyboards are hard and don't bend. For this reason, bodyboarders call surfboards "hardboards."

Of all rad boards, bodyboards come in the most different sizes and shapes. Some have rounded noses, some have blunt noses, some have square tails, and some have curved tails. There are also big differences in weight, materials and quality of construction. There are so many choices that it's easy to get confused when shopping for your first board. Once again, it's best to go to a surfboard store or other specialty shop where a knowledgeable salesperson will be able to help you. Or you can look for the most recent issue of a magazine called *Body Boarding,* because it usually has an article on the newest boards available.

One board you should not buy is a styrofoam board. You have probably seen these boards at the beach.

They are the big white boards that a lot of little kids play on at the edge of the water. Styrofoam is the same lightweight material used to make ice chests and coolers. The problem with styrofoam is that it breaks easily and doesn't bend.

Styrofoam boards are lots of fun and you can learn how to catch and ride a wave with one. But if you're going to be serious about bodyboarding, you need a board that is durable and bends when you turn. Real bodyboards are made of polyethylene. They cost more than styrofoam boards, but they are worth it.

When picking out a bodyboard, size is the first thing to consider. Bodyboards are 18 to 24 inches wide, and 24 to 44 inches long. Most are between 33 and 43 inches long. To measure for the right size, stand the board on its tail on the floor. The nose of the board should come up to your belly button or a little farther. As for width, you should be able to carry the board under one arm, comfortably but snugly. If you are growing fast, you might want to buy a larger board that you can grow into.

The next thing to consider is the shape of the sides. To start, you want a board with rounded instead of straight sides. The rounded sides make the board easier to turn and are better for small waves, which is what you'll ride in the beginning.

Next, look for what's called the "wide-point" on the board. It's easy to find—it's where the board is widest. Compare several boards and you'll see that some boards are widest near the nose and some are widest nearer the tail. You'll want a board with the wide-point near the nose. These boards give you a steadier ride and will make learning a lot easier.

Board Stiffness

Some boards have a layer of plastic on the bottom. This is called "slick skin," and it makes the board faster and stiffer. Some stiffness is good, but avoid boards that are hard to bend. After all, bending a bodyboard helps you steer. Get a salesman to help you bend several boards. Take a board, put the tail on the floor, hold the nose up and gently push your knee into the center. The board shouldn't feel flimsy, but there should be some give to it.

There are lots of other things to learn about the design of a bodyboard. For example, boards have differently shaped sides, or "rails." Some also have "wingers," which means that the last few inches of the tail is about four inches narrower than the rest of the board. These kinds of differences can make buying a bodyboard very complicated, but any soft board with a slick skin bottom and some bend to it is good enough to learn on.

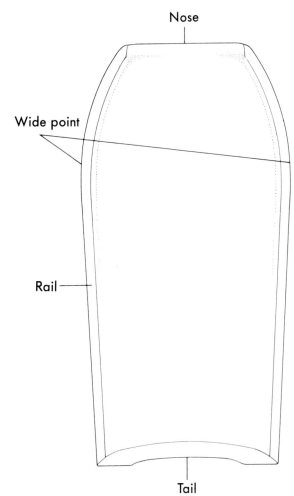

A typical bodyboard. Bodyboards come in many shapes and can be made of different materials, but they will have one thing in common—they are soft and flexible.

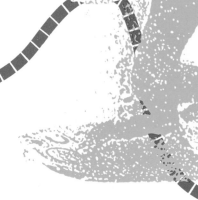

CHAPTER 15

MAKING WAVES AND BASIC MOVES

After you've bought a bodyboard, you're almost ready to hit the waves. First, though, there are some things to understand about the surf, which is where you'll be riding your board. The surf is what makes bodyboarding different from other rad board sports. In bodyboarding, you're propelled by a powerful, moving force: a wave.

Even a little wave can push you a long way on your bodyboard, which is exactly what you want the wave to do. But a strong wave can also hold you under the surface against your will. Whether you ride the wave or get pushed under it is determined by how you handle the wave. So it's important to understand the surf—and always treat it with respect.

Waves are formed by a combination of wind, currents and tide. Wind you already know about. That's air moving along the surface of the planet. Currents are little underwater rivers in which channels of water move through still water. The tide is a twice-a-day rise and fall of the ocean level as measured on the shore. Tides are caused by the moon, which is so close to the earth that its gravity actually pulls the surface of the sea toward it as it circles the planet.

When you combine those three forces, you get water moving toward the beach in waves. A wave begins far out in the ocean as a swell, or a rounded bulge in the water. The low dip in the water just in front of a wave is called the trough or trench. The edges of the wave are the wave's shoulders.

As a wave moves toward the beach and grows bigger, the crest on top begins to curl and form a lip. The wave curls more and more until finally the lip falls forward. This is when the wave breaks.

If the lip of the wave falls way out in front of the wave as it breaks, the wave is said to have a pitching lip. Hot bodyboarders love pitching lips because they can do rad tricks on them. They also like riding inside the wall of water that falls in front of the wave when it breaks. This wall is called the curtain, and the space inside the curtain is the tube or barrel. A wave that forms a big tube is said to be a hollow wave.

Big tubes often are formed by waves that break on rock or coral reefs. These are called reef breaks, and they are dangerous. Even good bodyboarders can get scraped and bruised in reef breaks.

For your first try at bodyboarding, find a beach with a smooth, sandy shore and gentle waves. Stay away from rocks and reefs, and save the big waves for later when you've mastered the basic skills.

Don't forget to take a buddy with you. You should never swim or bodyboard alone—you always want someone there in case you get into trouble and need help. The ocean is a big, powerful force and can be very dangerous. You don't ever want to face it alone.

Besides taking a friend and your board with you, you'll need one other piece of gear: swim fins. Without fins, you can't get up the speed to catch waves. To learn more about types of fins, see the section on parts and accessories in Chapter 17.

Getting Ready

Before you launch your new board, be sure to wax it. Bodyboards have smooth surfaces and can get slippery in the water. A waxed board is easier to grip. Bubble Gum and BZ are two common brands of bodyboard wax. If you have to buy surfing wax, get

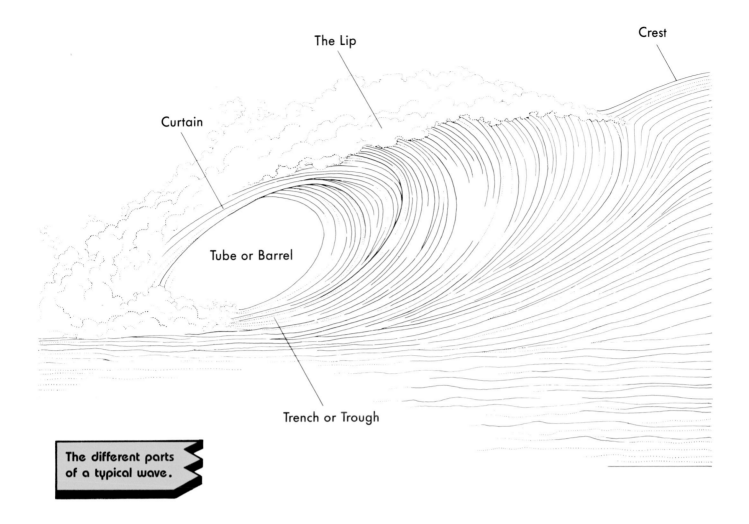

Crest

The Lip

Curtain

Tube or Barrel

Trench or Trough

The different parts of a typical wave.

winter wax, which is softer and easy to spread.

Spread the wax heaviest along the rails near the nose, where you'll be putting your hands. Cover the deck with a lighter coat. Waxing the deck not only gives you traction, but it also prolongs the life of the board by keeping water out of the surface. Use the edge of the wax stick for thick coats and the flat side for wide, thin coats.

You'll eventually develop your own style of waxing. Pro riders like Ben Severson, who rivals Mike Stewart as the best bodyboarder in the world, hardly waxes the deck at all. Severson feels that a waxed deck keeps him from moving around easily. Others such as Danny Kim, a pro who has bodyboarded for more than 10 years, prefers lots of wax because he sometimes stands on the board like a surfer. How you wax the board depends on your style. It's up to you to experiment and decide.

After you've waxed up, it's time to put your fins on. They should be snug without cramping your feet. Even if they fit right, fins are hard to walk in. It's easiest to put them on near the water so you don't have to walk too far in them. They will also help protect your feet against broken shells, rocks and other hard-to-see things in the water.

Learning the Basic Position

You'll want to get the feel of the board in shallow water before you paddle all the way out to the surf. As you lie on it, try shifting your weight around to see how the board responds.

Now is the time to learn the basic bodyboarding position. Lie on the board on your belly. Grab the nose with both hands and rest your weight on your elbows. Be sure that your hips are out of the water and up on the board. Now, alternate lifting and lowering your legs slightly to see how it affects the way you float. If you're in the correct position, your back will be arched sharply.

Look at photographs of top pros such as Mike Stewart and Ben Severson. If you ride the way they do, you'll have your elbows and arms up on the nose, and your hips will be well out of the water.

Hold that image in your mind—that's how you want to look, now that it's finally time to hit the waves!

Scouting the Water

Before you head into the water and paddle out to catch a wave, scout the water. Walk along the beach and look for a place where there are fewer waves. That will be a good place to swim out because you won't have to work hard and tire yourself. Channels, where the water is deeper, are usually good. Channels are sometimes easy to spot because the water is darker in that area.

Also notice which direction the waves are breaking. You'll want to "take off" and ride the waves in the same direction they are breaking.

After you've practiced the basic body position, you can paddle or flutter-kick your board out from the shore.

Paddling moves you faster, but it also takes more energy. Try alternating between the two so that you can rest your arms and legs.

Most good bodyboarders paddle for short bursts of speed and kick for prolonged efforts. "Your leg muscles are stronger and keep you going longer," says champion Mike Stewart. "But on a last-ditch effort you do both—whatever it takes to get out of the way of a big wave."

When you paddle, slide forward on your board so that your hands reach well out in front of the board. Take long, strong strokes. When you kick, slide back so that your hips rest on the back edge of the board. Hold on to the nose, resting on your forearms. Kick just below the surface and try not to splash. It's okay to break the surface, but a lot of splashing means that you're wasting energy. Again, take slow powerful strokes.

Avoid paddling through the surf on your way out. Wait for a lull between waves. Going out through big waves will just slow you up and make you tired. Save your strength for riding the waves back in!

A bodyboarder in the basic position on his bodyboard cuts across the face of a wave.

The Duck Dive: Push the nose of your bodyboard below the water. Then use your knee to shove the tail down. The bodyboard will go under water and take you with it.

Turning Turtle and the Duck Dive

Sometimes it's impossible to miss going through pounding waves on your way out. When a big one heads your way, you can do one of two things to avoid getting knocked off your board or pushed back toward the beach: Flip upside down under your board or dive beneath the surface.

Flipping upside down is called "turtling" or "turning turtle." This is an old surfing maneuver. You just turn over in the water with your board above you to cushion the impact of the crashing wave. Hold the nose firmly and dip it a little deeper than the rest of the board.

Diving beneath the surface is called the "duck dive." Most good riders prefer this technique for avoiding

surf—it takes less time and energy than turtling. To do a duck dive you have to push your board beneath the surface. Wait until the wave is almost on you, then grab the rails eight or ten inches from the tip of the nose. Push the nose under the water and make the tail follow it down by shoving it down with your knee. Both you and your board will go below the wave.

When Mike Stewart duck dives in the big surf of Hawaii, he angles the nose up a bit so that it faces directly into the crashing wave. That way the board is streamlined into the oncoming whitewater.

Stay submerged long enough to let the wave pass—a few seconds is all it takes. Then lift the nose to come back up, avoiding the most turbulent part of the wave. Don't stay under too long. Paddle out to where the waves swell for a few seconds before breaking. Now all that's left to do is catch the right one and ride it!

Bodyboarders can share waves because their boards are soft. Surfboards, which are hard, can be dangerous to others if a surfer loses control.

Catching a Wave

When a nice big wave comes your way, turn toward shore and use one hand to paddle. Hold the nose with the other hand. Meanwhile, kick with both feet. Just as the wave reaches you, push the nose of the board downward a little with the hand that's not paddling. This lets the wave catch the nose of the board and pull it along. Be careful not to push the nose under water, which is called "pearling." Timing is critical. If you push down too late, you'll either miss the wave or get launched by the curl at the top, which is called the lip. A lip launch may send you crashing down the face of the wave. As soon as you've caught the wave, lift your legs out of the water a little. That way you'll have less resistance, or "drag."

Starting off on a wave is called "dropping in," the same term skateboarders and snowboarders use for starting on half-pipes. Dropping in gives you a real killer feeling. One second you're kicking hard and barely moving; the next second you're shooting along the face of a wave.

If the wave is big and steep, you may have to pull up on the nose once you've dropped in. On a really steep wave you could find yourself out of the water in a "free fall," or "air drop." If this happens, don't fight it; just try to land on one of the back corners of your board. If you lose control completely and wipe out, let go of the board and simply try to land as gently as possible.

You may have just the opposite problem—you can't seem to catch any wave. In that case, you may be too far out. Try moving closer to shore.

Once you've dropped in, you'll have to decide whether you're going to ride to the left or right on the wave. You may have decided this while you were still on the shore, watching which way the waves were breaking. Either way, the next step is to learn how to guide the board.

Turning and Trimming

Once you've dropped in, you have to turn one way or the other to ride across the face of the wave—which is called "going down the line." The direction depends on which way the wave is breaking and where the strongest part of the wave is.

Let's say you want to go left. First, slide back and toward the inside rail, which is the side closest to the wave. On a left turn, this is your left side. Your left hip should be over the left back corner of the board. Now grab the front left corner of the board with your left hand and pull up gently. At the same time, lean to the left and pull up with your right hand on the right rail about a foot back from the front of the board. This tilts the board to the left and makes you go in that direction. If you get a good left turn going, the board will slice through the water on its left edge.

Riding on one edge helps you go faster and carve turns. Carving is just as important in bodyboarding as it is in snowboarding. Carving means the board runs through the water on its edge in a slightly curved path. The secret to carving is to pull the nose up slightly. The bend that you give the board makes it turn naturally on its edge.

Foot and Hand Aids

Many beginners find it hard to keep one edge in the water for a long time. The board seems too wobbly. You can solve this problem by dragging your inside foot in the water behind you. If you're going left across the face of the wave, you would drag your left foot.

One pro rider, J. P. Patterson, uses an odd technique of dragging his outside hand in the water. Patterson, known for his wild antics on big waves, is famous for his unique style. Other pros call Patterson's way of riding "the wounded duck style" because Patterson looks like a duck dragging a broken wing in the water.

Dragging a foot or hand in the water adds stability just as the tail of a kite helps the kite fly with more stability. It also slows you down. Most good riders believe that as you improve, you should break this habit and learn how to ride on the edges of the board without any aids.

Bottom Turns—Stretching Your Ride Out

If you've dropped in straight instead of on a turn, you should do a "bottom turn." This move, which is the first step to more advanced maneuvers, is simply a sharp turn at the bottom of the wave. To do one, you slide back and over to one side of the board, pulling up on the outside rail as you lean. This will make you turn just as it did up on the wave.

Anytime you come out of a turn, slide back toward the center and front of the board. This not only gets you ready for the next turn, it also gives you an extra boost by letting your board spring out of the turn.

You'll find that moving forward on the board gives you more speed but less control in turning. Conversely, moving back over the tail makes the board easier to maneuver but slows you down. It's all a trade-off. Through practice, you'll learn how and when to strike a balance between the two.

Once you've made your turn, continue riding across the wave face on the board's inside edge. This is called "trimming." Whenever you're trimming, the board should be sliding through the water at its fastest speed. At this point, don't pull up on the nose. The board's naturally curved bottom will conform to the curved surface of the wave. You can increase your speed by tapping into the two strongest parts of a wave: the upper third, which is the steepest part, and the trough, which is the front edge at the bottom of the wave.

On weak or mushy waves, champion bodyboarder Mike Stewart waits until just after the wave breaks to do any fancy turns or maneuvers. "The wave usually kind of crumbles at first," he says. "Then there's a burst of speed. That's when you want to do your maneuver."

If you've done everything right, you'll soon be ripping along the wave, screaming your lungs out with joy.

Of course, you may not like the wave you've caught or it may "close out." If so, there are several ways to get off the wave. Both methods are called "pull-outs." One is simply to go over the top. To do that, you do a sharp turn in the direction you're going down the wave. The wave should then just pass under you.

If you're too far down on the wave to go over the top, you'll have to pull out through the face. This is

This bodyboarder shows the correct hand, arm and body positions to make a perfect right turn. Riding on one edge helps you go faster.

called a "Hawaiian pull-out." To do one, arc the board back into the face as sharply as you can. At the same time, push the nose deep into the water, slide up on your board and duck your head at the last second and dive into the wave.

It takes a lot of strength to pull a board through a passing wave. You'll have to hold on tight and keep the nose pointed into the wave. You don't want to let the flat surface of the board get caught by the rushing water. After the wave has passed, you can get back to the surface by sliding your board under you, lifting the nose and letting it float you up.

Cutbacks

If you hit part of a wave that's too mushy to ride, carve a "cutback." This move cannot only put you back in the more powerful part of the wave, but it's also a lot of fun to ride.

A cutback is just another form of a basic turn, except it's done so sharply that you almost completely reverse direction. Some bodyboarders like to use cutbacks to bank off the foam or lip of a wave.

You need as much speed as possible to do a cutback. One way to get a little extra speed is to pump your head forward several times like a pigeon does when it walks. Also, try to stay on the upper half of the wave so that you'll have the room and speed to do the cutback.

Let's say you want to do a cutback while going left on a wave. The cutback will be to the right. First, put your right hip over the right rear corner of the board. Next, slide both hands up to the corner of the nose and pull back hard. This will turn the board. At the same time, push down with your elbows and lean to the right.

Jay Reale, from Ocean City, Maryland, is one of the few pros originally from the East Coast. He writes in *Body Boarding* magazine that for a quick cutback, "You'll need to bow the board a little more. . . Use the spring, or recoil, of the board to come out of the turn with maximum speed, and then return your hands and body immediately to their original positions."

Naturally, a cutback will slow you down. You can get back some of your lost speed by moving back toward the center and front of the board again. You'll regain even more speed when you catch the strong part of the wave again.

Of course, cutbacks and bottom turns are good for more than simply getting to a better part of the wave. They're also fun. Whenever you do them, go for it— shoot some spray with your board, scream and yell— let loose.

Keep practicing bottom turns and cutbacks until you can do them smoothly and sharply. Then you'll be ready to try some of the really rad bodyboard moves.

CHAPTER 16

n bodyboarding, as in skateboarding and snowboarding, the really tough stunts are simply more complex versions of a handful of fundamental tricks. As a beginner, you should first learn a few off-the-lip maneuvers, ''spinners'' and ''el rollos.''

An off-the-lip maneuver is just what it sounds like: You ride the board up the face of the wave and then take off from the top of the wave. To go off the lip, pick a spot on the wave that looks like it's about to break. The steepest section is usually the best place.

First, carve a bottom turn and aim for the part of the lip that you've picked out. As you climb the face, keep down the nose of your board and the outside rail (the edge facing the beach). Just before you reach the lip, pull up a little on the nose. Having the nose bent back will help you bounce off the lip. Keep your arms

extended so that when you hit the lip you can recoil by bending your elbows. If you hit the right spot, you'll fly into the air and then back down into the wave. Now that's hot!

With practice, you should be able to land on the wave and continue on down the line, spinning off-the-lip maneuvers the entire length of the wave as it heads for the beach.

A trick that looks just as awesome as an off-the-lip maneuver is the spinner, also called belly spinner or 360. Again, this trick looks just like it sounds: You and your board spin around on the surface of the water. You can do a spinner on any part of the wave while going in any direction.

Aided Spinners

If you're going to the right, it's easiest to spin clockwise, or to the right. That way, you take advantage of the natural force of the wave to help turn you around. If you're going left, spin counterclockwise. These are called ''forward spinners.''

To start a clockwise spinner, lift both legs out of the water and drop your right hand into the water. Dragging your hand will start the spin. Use of your hand makes the move an ''aided spinner.''

As you drop your hand, throw your head to the right and lean forward and to the right. Keep the left edge of your board high so that it doesn't catch in the water. As you start to spin, bend your knees and bring your feet almost up to your rear. That should help you spin faster. To do a forward belly spinner on the left, you do all the same moves in reverse. For example, you start the spin by dropping your left hand into the water.

On the first few tries, it will be hard to finish the spin. One way to stop is to drop your legs in the water when you're about two-thirds of the way around. That will help you complete the rotation. As you get better, you can wait longer to drop your legs.

Unaided and Reverse Spinners

After you get better at spinners, try spinning without out dragging your hand in the water. These are

A bodyboarder uses the edge of his board to cut back on the lip of a wave.

"unaided spinners." You'll look a lot smoother if you can spin no-handed.

It's also possible to do a spinner in the opposite direction, but it's a lot harder. This is called a "reverse spinner." If you're going to the right on a wave, a reverse spinner would be to the left, or in a counterclockwise direction. Reverse spinners are harder because your legs and the tail of your board have more of a tendency to catch in the water and stop your spin.

To do a reverse spinner, you simply switch your movements to the other side of the board. For example, if you're going to the right, drag your left hand and throw your body and head to the left. Remember, you have to throw your weight harder than in a forward spinner.

If you have trouble doing reverse spinners, practice on short, mushy waves. It's easier when the waves aren't too steep and fast. Don't worry. You'll eventually get it, especially when you get the hang of twisting your body. This is called "body English."

El Rollos

Another move that takes some know-how is the "el rollo." This is a really rad trick. An el rollo is a corkscrew-shaped roll. Ideally, your el rollo occurs at the moment when you're more out of the water and above the wave than in it—sort of like an aerial, but with an extra twist. The first time you do one, you'll feel like a real champion bodyboarder.

To pull off an el rollo, you need a fairly hollow wave. Othewise, you end up doing an "el floppo," which is a sloppy el rollo. You need to pick a point on the wave where it's starting to break. As the wave swells and moves toward you, do a bottom turn for speed and aim for the lip.

Just as you hit the lip of the wave, which will launch you forward, twist your body and your board in the

An el rollo happens more out of the water and above it, than in it. It's the body-boarder's way to grab air!

direction that the wave is breaking. After bouncing off of the lip of the wave, while you and your board are momentarily airborne, roll from stomach to back to stomach. Before you know it, the wave is crashing behind you and you're riding out the foam.

If you're on a mushy wave, you may have to give a little extra effort. Ben Severson, who is one of the best el rollo riders alive, aims for the edge of the whitewater, extends his arms and twists hard at the waist. Those little extras help him roll better on a little wave.

Roll in the direction that the lip is pitching. Flow with the wave. If you're going left on the wave, your left shoulder will lead your right shoulder through the roll. Keep your hands in the usual trim position: right hand on the board's nose; left hand at about the mid-point of the left rail (reverse for going right).

Your body will be pitched toward the shore, which is good. Most often you'll land on the top half of the wave. However, in the best el rollos, you land in the trough.

Just before landing, extend your arms along the board to act as shock absorbers. Be careful not to pearl. Lift the nose of your board and try to land on the inside rail. If you're going left, the inside rail is the left rail. If you do the el rollo well, you can continue going down the line, hitting the wave with el rollos over and over as it rushes for the sand!

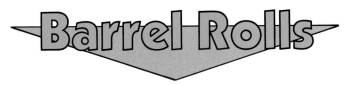

A "barrel roll" is just like an el rollo except you roll inside the "tube," the hollow interior of a wave. For a barrel roll, you want to aim just behind the hook of the wave. That means you have to hit the lip a moment later than you would in doing an el rollo.

Barrel rolls are an advanced move and tough to do. Rolling inside a breaking wave is scary. Lots of bodyboarders chicken out about halfway through the flip. You can't do that. If you want to complete the maneuver, you have to ride it out.

When you come down, it's crucial to land on the water on your inside rail. Once you've set your edge, you have to push down on your outside rail to stop your roll and to keep from going around again. Often the wave will crash on you before you can finish a barrel roll. You may have to do a Hawaiian pull-out to avoid being pummeled by the wave. For this reason, it's very hard to continue down the line after a barrel roll.

You need really good hollow waves for barrel rolls. Hawaii is the best place, but California and the East Coast sometimes have the right waves, too. The same is true for tube riding, which is the ultimate in bodyboarding.

Tube riding is one of the many reasons lots of people like bodyboarding better than surfing. A tube—or barrel, as it's sometimes called—is the hollow tunnel that is formed when a wave rolls over as it breaks.

On a bodyboard, you can fit into more tubes and ride them longer than you can on a surfboard, because you're lying down instead of standing up. That lets you ride smaller tubes with more stability.

Mike Stewart calls tube riding the ultimate in bodyboarding. "In a tube you can do things that are almost like time-machine maneuvers," he says. "If you do a 360 in a tube, for instance, not only can you see where you're going but also where you've been. It's a real rush to pivot around and see parts of the wave behind you'd never see ordinarily."

But you need to be a good bodyboarder to take on waves that are hollow enough for tube riding. If you get caught inside a monster, you can get ground up like hamburger. To avoid getting mashed, you need speed and a good strong trim. If you catch a tubed wave and find yourself riding in the barrel, don't try cutting or turning. Turns will just slow you down and may prevent you from getting out before the tube collapses.

Put your weight on the inside rail to set a hard edge in the water. In really hollow waves, keep your weight on the back inside corner of the board and keep your inside leg straight and in the water to help hold the edge. As you approach the bottom of the wave, quickly slide forward on the board to increase your speed.

Keep your eyes open and be determined to make it out. Kainoa McGee, a Hawaiian who is a super-hot tube rider, says in Body Boarding magazine that "one of the most important things to remember is to look straight ahead, focusing your attention on your goal, the end of the barrel."

If you look ahead and keep your speed up, and if the tube doesn't collapse, you'll get out O.K. And then you'll understand why so many bodyboarders want to live in California and Hawaii, near the truly rad tubes.

A tube is formed when a wave breaks, and the lip and curtain create a round hollow. Because bodyboards are short, and you ride on them lying down, they're perfect for tube riding. Some bodyboarders think tube riding is the ultimate!

Drop-Knee Riding

If you've seen many photographs or videos of body-boarders, you've probably seen drop-knee riders. These are the bodyboarders who kneel on the middle of the board with one leg and set the foot of the other leg flat near the nose.

Drop-knee riding used to be called the "Jack Stance," after Jack Lindholm, a top pro who is credited with inventing it. Every good bodyboarder eventually wants to try drop-knee riding. This style frees your hands, lets your pump your board for speed and gets you in a higher position that is more like surfing.

Drop-knee riders do a lot of the same turns and tricks that regular riders do. However, some tricks—barrel rolls, for example—are virtually impossible in the drop-knee style. Other stunts aren't quite so difficult.

Getting into Position

One of the hardest parts of drop-knee riding is get-ting up on the board. You should practice on land before you try it in water. First, decide which foot is more comfortable in front.

Let's look at how a regular footer gets up. (If you're goofy-footed, follow the same instructions but use the opposite hands and feet.) As you drop in, grab the nose with your right hand and the middle of the left rail with your left hand. Then slide forward just a little bit on the board.

Next, put most of your weight on your right elbow on the board. Then, lift your rear enough to bring your right knee up on the deck. Almost immediately, bring your left leg out of the water, swinging it out to the left side to keep the fin out of the water. To put your foot up on the deck, you'll have to let go of the left rail long enough to swing your foot past it. The hard part is doing all that in one smooth motion.

Another way to get into the drop-knee stance is to put both hands on the nose and then bring both knees up onto the deck. Then you can swing the front foot up onto the nose.

Drop knee riders do a lot of the same turns and tricks that regular bodyboarders do.

Turning

Turning in a drop-knee position is harder than turning while you're lying flat on the board because you're less stable. To start a turn, grab the outside rail about halfway down the edge of the board. Drop your inside hand into the water—this gives you a pivot to turn around. As you drop your hand, weight your knee and heel and lean into the turn.

The harder you lean, the sharper you'll turn. Finish out the arc that you've started by twisting your shoulders into the turn. That should help the board follow your body around.

Riding in the drop-knee position takes a lot of strength in your kneeling leg. You use this leg to force the board around. For instance, if you're making a front-side cutback (facing the wave and turning away from the wave), you use your kneeling leg to press the board through the turn. On a back-side turn, the back leg digs the back outside rail into the water, and the rest of the board pivots around it.

Standing Up

A few really rad riders can stand on both feet while riding, like a surfer on a surfboard. This group includes Danny Kim and Kevin Cerv, two professionals who consistently finish in the top 10 in national rankings.

Kim has been a stand-up rider for more than 10 years. Cerv is probably the best bodyboarder in California. Both riders stand on many of their rides. This is a very unstable position, but they can even make turns standing up.

Not everyone wants to ride standing up, though. Some bodyboarders argue that if you want to stand up, you should take up surfing instead of bodyboarding. ''Riding prone is faster, more functional and also is the essence of bodyboarding,'' says Mike Stewart, who rides drop-knee and standing less than 1% of the time.

But you should follow your own wishes. Some riders believe that riding in drop-knee and standing positions are the ultimate in bodyboarding, even if they're a little hard to do. If you have trouble learning either style, don't give up. With practice, you can do anything.

CHAPTER 17

PARTS AND ACCESSORIES

When it comes to equipment, bodyboarding is a very simple sport. Most of the time all you need is a board, fins and a good sense of balance. However, certain water and weather conditions sometimes demand one or two extra pieces of gear.

Let's look at fins first. There are two basic kinds of fins: diving fins and open-heel fins. Diving fins are like slippers with super long toes. They aren't especially good for bodyboarding. They are really made for scuba divers who have to walk over coral or rocks to get to a dive site. Also, the blades are too long. Open-heel fins work much better for bodyboarding because they fit your foot snugly and the straps make them more likely to stay on your foot in the surf. Diving fins don't usually fit as tightly and can easily get knocked off in a wipe-out.

Fins also come in lots of shapes and sizes. Some have squared-off toes, some are V-shaped and others have more rounded toes. Generally, longer fins have either slightly rounded, curved or square noses. Longer and wider fins are usually faster once you get moving, but it takes longer to build up speed. For quicker starts in big waves, use shorter fins, which often are wedge- or V-shaped.

The important things to look for in bodyboarding fins are fit, comfort, short blades, and a hole for water to drain out of when they're on your feet. If you're worried about losing your fins, get a pair of fin tethers. These are nylon or rubber cords that connect fin straps to cuffs that go around your ankles.

Similar cords called leashes can be used to keep you from losing your bodyboard. Some bodyboarders connect leashes to their wrists, while others attach them to their ankles. Leashes are good things to have. If you ever get hurt while bodyboarding, a leash will keep your board nearby so you can use it as a life preserver. Sometimes a leash can be used to help control the board. Keith Sasaki, a pro rider from Hawaii, attaches his leash to his wrist and uses it to lift the nose of his board while he's riding in drop-knee position.

A few bodyboarders use handles and skegs on their boards. A handle can come in handy for turning. Skegs are six-inch fins that can be attached to the bottom of a board. They make you more stable by keeping the board from drifting to the right or left. Skegs can also help you hold your edge when you're turning and trimming. But they also slow you down and keep you from doing belly spinners.

If you have trouble holding onto your board in surf, you may want to add some "traction surface." This is a thin foam with a sticky back. You put it where your hands grip the board—on the bottom of the nose and under the rails. It has the same purpose as "griptape" for skateboards, but it's spongier and less coarse. Traction surface comes in different widths and shapes, and you can cut it to whatever size and shape you need.

Board bags are another handy item. They're usually made out of nylon and have extra pockets for carrying accessories. Most have both handles and shoulder straps so that you can carry them by hand or on your back. Some also have a mesh bottom for carrying damp wetsuits.

Wetsuits are essential for bodyboarding in cold water. They are also very expensive. It's easy to spend $200 on a wetsuit. The arms and legs of wetsuits come in different lengths. Short sleeves and legs are good for fall and spring bodyboarding. For winter water, you will need a wetsuit with long legs and sleeves. In cool water in summer, you may want to wear a wetsuit vest.

For added warmth, fin socks are a good buy. These are socks worn inside your fins, made out of either nylon or neoprene (the same stuff wetsuits are made out of). Fin socks also help protect your feet against rough ocean bottoms. At $20 or less, they're not a bad deal.

Gloves help keep your hands warm, and they give your hands extra paddling power for faster take-off speeds. For this reason, there's webbing between the fingers. Gloves are made out of different combinations of rubber and nylon. Look for gloves with sticky rubber on the palms to help grip the board. Gloves cost $10 to $30.

Once you have all the gear you need, there's not much you have to do to maintain it. Be sure to keep everything out of direct sunlight as much as possible. Sunlight can destroy neoprene. And you should always wash the salt water off all your equipment in a shower or with a garden hose.

Bodyboards can take lots of abuse, but that's no reason not to protect your investment. There are several things you can do to prolong the life of your board. One, don't drag it. Two, keep it out of direct sunlight. Three, don't set items on top of it. Four, rinse it off after use. Five, store it in a board bag. And finally, don't jam the rails into the ground.

Over time, even well-protected bodyboards lose their camber, which is the built-in bend in the board from the nose to the tail. But don't worry. That's one more advantage to bodyboarding: If your board is damaged or flattens out, it doesn't cost a whole lot of money to get another one. That's one advantage that surfers don't have.

CHAPTER 18

t's not hard to find a beach for bodyboarding. Bodyboarders don't need giant waves. You can have lots of fun even on waves only a couple feet high. In fact, small waves are best to start on. You're less likely to hurt yourself on little swells. Look for a beach with gently rolling waves. You want waves that break diagonally toward the shore instead of waves that break straight into the beach.

It's important to be careful where you bodyboard because moving water is very powerful. When you fall off your board—it's called "wiping out"—a big wave can twist and turn you and slam you against the bottom. It can also hold you under water longer than you can hold your breath.

When you wipe out, roll with the wave and do not dive toward the bottom, so that you don't hurt your head, neck or spine. When you wipe out in larger waves and you have to dive into the trough, make it a shallow dive.

Be particularly careful to avoid big waves that break close to shore. Waves that break near shore are called "shore breaks." You can get pounded in big shore breaks. Surfers and swimmers have suffered broken necks and backs in such conditions.

Stay away from crowded beaches with lots of fishermen, surfers and swimmers. If you don't, you may end up running into a surfboard, a fish hook, or another person. Also, practice safety and courtesy. One rule is that the first bodyboarder or surfer to catch a wave has the right-of-way, which means everyone else has to get out of his way. If you find yourself about to hit somebody, do a pull-out. It's better to let go of a good wave than to hurt yourself or someone else.

Bodyboarding Paradise

After you've bodyboarded for many years, you can begin thinking about going to the ultimate beaches—in Hawaii! This is where almost all the top pro bodyboarders live at least part of the year.

The island of Oahu in Hawaii is the most famous surfing and bodyboarding spot in the world. The north side of Oahu, called the North Shore, is the dream destination of practically every surfer and bodyboarder.

Waves on the North Shore can be as high as 60 feet because of the strong winds that blow there. Mike Stewart once saw the wind blow so strong on the North Shore that it lifted a bodyboarder out of the water. "He traveled 30 or 40 feet before the wind blew him into the back of a wave," Stewart recalls. "Who knows? Maybe you could actually get enough wind to fly all the way to the beach."

Pipeline is one of the North Shore's best known beaches. Songs have been written about it and movies have been filmed at Pipeline. In winter, the faces of waves are routinely 25 feet high or bigger. Another famous winter bodyboarding spot in Hawaii is the Waimea Shore Break. The waves there are a lot like those at Pipeline, which is right down the beach from Waimea.

On the other side of Oahu is Sandy Beach, another famous surfing beach. Summertime is the best season for big waves there, which get up to 10 feet or higher. The waves at Sandy Beach break with big tubes and steep faces for super-fast bodyboarding.

The West Coast

California has its share of great bodyboarding beaches, too. Probably the most famous is The Wedge, at Newport Beach south of Los Angeles. It's called The Wedge because of the way the waves break. A big rock jetty is built out into the ocean at a harbor entrance. Waves bounce off the jetty and run into other waves, making those waves bigger. In September and October, some waves are even ''triple overheads''— three times as tall as a grown person.

South of Los Angeles are excellent bodyboarding beaches. Huntington Beach was once called the surfing capital of the United States. Laguna Beach has consistently good waves, and San Clemente has waves that are gentle and smooth, even when they're running high. Farther south, there are many good beaches near San Diego.

Other Hot Spots

The East Coast is not without some good places to bodyboard. In Florida, Daytona Beach and the Cape Canaveral area often have good surf. The Outer Banks in North Carolina, Virginia Beach in Virginia, and Ocean City in Maryland can also be good. Other places with big surf include the New Jersey shore and Long Island in New York, which has especially good conditions on the south shore.

You can also bodyboard at artificial wave pools. These are giant swimming pools with big flaps or some other device at one end to make waves. Artificial waves can be four feet or higher. Unfortunately, there are only a few wave pools around the country that allow bodyboarders. These include water parks in Tempe, Arizona; Allentown, Pennsylvania; Irvine, Palm Springs; and Clovis, California.

CHAPTER 19

COMPETITIONS

■■■■■■■■■■■■■■■■■

It's only natural that someday you will want to enter some kind of rad board contest. As you improve in skateboarding, snowboarding or bodyboarding, you will probably want to test yourself against other people.

Competitions aren't hard to find. National organizations in all three sports hold contests around the country. Of course, many competitions will be far from where you live. It's fun to travel across the country to a faraway contest, but it's also expensive. Look for contests near your home, and keep practicing until you are good enough to win money at competitions. That's how the pros afford to go to meets all over the country.

That day may actually be closer than you think. Some of the best riders are young and have only a few years of experience. Danny Way became a pro skateboarder when he was 15, about five years earlier than many skaters enter the pros. Today, he rivals Tony Hawk as the most famous skater alive, even though he's six years younger than Hawk.

In bodyboarding, Kainoa McGee of Hawaii entered his first contest at age 10. At 16, he placed third in a national contest and was pictured on the cover of a magazine. Many people believe that McGee will someday rival Mike Stewart as the king of bodyboarding.

Who knows—perhaps you'll become a rad board star one day. But first you'll have to win some contests. So start practicing.

Skateboarding Competitions

The Big Time

Competitive skateboarding is getting very fancy and fun to watch. Each year the skill level of the riders rises sharply. If you go to a regional or national competition, you'll see professional riders doing more rad tricks than you'll ever see back home.

This makes competitive skateboarding exciting for spectators. But if you want to compete in regional and national contests, you will have to spend lots of time practicing. In fact, training to get good enough to win these contests is almost a full-time job.

One reason is money. Winners of national contests win up to $10,000 each, and sometimes the winners have sponsors who double their winnings. So top skateboarders can earn up to $20,000 in one contest. These high stakes can make skateboarding very competitive. Fortunately, though, not all contests are that hard.

In Your Own Home Town

At many local contests, there are non-professionals (amateurs, who don't earn money from skateboarding) and even skaters who've never competed before. Many times, competitors compete for plaques or trophies instead of money. In other contests, you can win skateboards, skateboard parts and t-shirts. These are the contests where you want to start, since they are much easier and more open to beginners.

The typical contest is usually judged by a panel of five judges. The judges give each skater a score of 1 to 100 based on how well they think the skater performed. To get a skater's final score, the highest and lowest of the five scores are thrown out, and then the remaining three scores are averaged.

Before you enter a competition, you'll have to decide which events you would do best in. There are usually four to choose from: mini-ramp, street style, vertical ramp and freestyle.

Mini-Ramp Events

In the mini-ramp event, skaters do ramp tricks on half-pipes four to six feet high. The mini-ramp is one of the best events to enter as a first-time competitor. You can do well by just sticking to the basic tricks like grinds and rock 'n' roll's. If it's your first contest, think seriously about entering the mini-ramp event.

Some contests have variations on the mini-ramp. Sometimes skaters compete on a ''spine ramp,'' for instance. A spine ramp is formed by putting two half-pipes back to back so that there's a ''spine,'' or narrow divider, between the pair of ramps. Skaters do tricks on one half-pipe, go up and over the spine and then do tricks on the other half-pipe. Competitions are also held on a ''Y ramp,'' which is three ramps put together in the shape of the letter Y.

When skaters move from one side of a spine or Y ramp to another, it's called a ''transfer.'' A good skater can do a 360 or another hot aerial in a transfer from one ramp to another. Done smoothly, those kinds of moves are real crowd pleasers.

Vertical Ramp Events

Vertical ramp events are like mini-ramp competitions, except that they are held on larger half-pipes. The ramps are up to 12 feet tall and have ''vert''—a straight up and down section about 12 to 18 inches tall at each of the two top edges. Competitors on the vertical ramps generally do fancier tricks. Because the ramps are bigger, you can skate faster and get a lot more air.

In both mini-ramp and vertical ramp events, competitors usually get two runs of 45 seconds each. The judges score each rider on his best run. If there are lots of skaters competing, there may be three rounds. The first round will be a qualifying round, in which the best half of all the riders will be choosen to go on to the next round, which is called the semi-finals. Half of the skaters will be chosen from the semi-finals to go on to the final round, which will decide the champion.

Sometimes riders will compete ''head to head,'' which means that two skaters ride at the same time and their performances are compared to each other. The rider with the better performance moves on to compete head-to-head with another skater. This continues until all the skaters are eliminated except one—the winner.

Three skaters wearing safety gear get ready to drop in on a vertical ramp event.

In other contests, there is a "jam format," which means that riders go one at a time and take as much time as they like. Each rider usually takes four runs and is scored on his best three of the four. The winner is the skater with the best scores.

In any format, ramp contests are cool to watch, especially if the pros are competing. There's nothing like the sight of a super-hot vert skater such as Gator Mark Anthony or Christian Hosoi barging the ramp— jargon for going really fast—and sailing eight or nine feet above the coping.

Street Style

Street style events are run much like mini-ramp and vertical events, except that competitors take a little more time—from 50 seconds to a minute, depending on the course.

Street style courses are usually laid out in an area about 150 feet by 180 feet, with one or more obstacles. In the center there's usually a ramp shaped like a rectangular or triangular pyramid with the top cut off. Often there is a metal rail running down one edge, like a hand rail running down a staircase. Skaters do aerials off the sides of this center piece. The really good skaters also do grinds and other stunts on the hand rail. It's awesome to watch pros Tom Knox or Steve Caballero grind all the way down a 20-foot-long rail.

Many times there are other obstacles in a street style course. There may be a quarter-pipe or a launch ramp, a parking curb, a park bench, a picnic table, a sidewalk for doing ollies, or a slider rail, which is a metal or plastic pipe for grinding.

The idea of a street style course is to make the obstacles much like those that you encounter on the streets. At the professional level, there may even be a car next to a launch ramp for the really good skaters to jump over.

Freestyle

Freestyle events, on the other hand, are held on smooth, flat pavement free of all obstacles. Freestyle skaters do as much as they can with only their boards— clean and simple.

Like the other events, the typical freestyle event is judged by a panel. Each competitor gets 90 seconds (pros get two minutes) to do a routine. Competitors often choreograph, or coordinate, their routines to music, just like ice skaters skate to music.

Putting a freestyle routine to music takes hard work. Kevin Harris, who is one of the world's best freestylers,

often practices a routine to one song 20 or 30 times a day, playing the same song over and over. He works on the routine for three or four months before a contest, because freestyle judges don't evaluate skaters on who does the hardest tricks. They judge them on who skates best to the music.

The Sound of Music

Music is very much a part of all skateboarding competitions. It is generally played in the background on big speakers, giving skaters a little extra energy and a beat to move to.

There is also generally a commentator announcing the event through loud speakers. The commentator describes each skater's moves while the skater is performing. The music and the commentary make for a charged, exciting atmosphere. You don't even have to skate to have fun at a contest.

Where to Find Contests

There are so many skateboard contests that they are easy to find. Look for announcements or advertisements for contests in skateboard magazines. (Check the appendix in the back of this book for a list of magazines.)

Another good source is the National Skateboarding Association. The NSA will lead you to your state's skateboarding association, which can provide information on local contests. Also, if you join the NSA, you get a newsletter that tells you about contests. For an additional $15 a year, you can get insurance that covers medical bills if you get hurt at an NSA-sponsored contest.

Snowboarding competitions are also becoming very popular and intensely competitive. For good reason: Sometimes there's big prize money for the winners.

It may sound odd, but many snowboarders do not

accept money for winning contests. Snowboarding may someday become an Olympic sport. The Olympics are supposed to be only for amateurs, athletes who don't win money. Some snowboarders hope they will remain eligible if and when the Olympics feature snowboarding. For this reason, the prizes at amateur contests may include plaques, trophies and snowboarding equipment instead.

If you're a beginning snowboarder, winning money won't matter to you right now anyway. You'll have to practice hard and long before you can think about beating any of the professional riders. In the meantime, you can start competing against other beginners.

Snowboarding contests are now held around the country for both pro and amateur riders. The way to find them is to look for announcements in any of the snowboarding magazines.

The Slalom

Most snowboarding contests have three events. In the "slalom," snowboarders weave through poles stuck about 15 feet apart in the snow. These poles are called "gates." Each run is timed, and the snowboarder who goes through the gates in the shortest time is the winner.

Slalom is exciting to watch. The gates are mounted on swivels, and a rider can knock a gate out of his way as he races past. Competitors usually wear plastic guards on their forearms for knocking the gates over. The gate bends at the swivels, slams into the snow and then snaps back upright after the rider passes.

A really good slalom rider gets a nice rhythm going as he flies gracefully through the gates. It's awesome to watch someone with the alpine skills of Jean Nerva, a French pro who rides on the Burton snowboarding team, as he knocks the gates over one after another with his arm guards. Slalom is a fun event for spectators.

Freestyle Events

Perhaps the coolest event of all is the freestyle competition. This takes place in the half-pipe, where riders do the most rad tricks and stunts imaginable.

A snowboarder weaves through a gate in a slalom event.

You should go to a national or international competition just to see the half-pipe contest. You'll see white-hot moves by riders such as Craig Kelly and Shaun Palmer, probably the two best freestylers in the world. This is the cutting edge of snowboarding, a showcase for the newest tricks. Competitors even invent new moves as they're warming up in the half-pipe, minutes before a freestyle event starts.

During the event, the best riders get as much as six or eight feet of air off the high walls of the half-pipe. You'll see them do incredible combinations of hand plants and flips off the lips of the walls. Hot stuff.

In freestyle events, a panel of judges evaluates each rider and awards him points. The judges award points based on how much air a rider gets, how original and difficult his tricks are, and how well he does them.

Freestyle contests are inspiring for any snowboarder to watch. You'll learn a lot about technique just by seeing how some of the really rad riders compete.

The Giant Slalom

The third event in most snowboarding contests is the giant slalom, also called the GS or the downhill. This can be as thrilling as the freestyle, only for a different reason: speed.

In the GS, there are only a half-dozen gates, and they're spaced about 100 feet apart. Again, the object is to weave through the gates, passing one on the right side, the next on the left side, and so on. But with so few gates and turns, riders go a lot faster in the GS than in the slalom.

In professional contests, riders often top 60 mph on giant slalom runs. Competitors usually wear helmets because a fall at that speed can be very serious.

Many times, though, GS contests are held on shorter courses where it's hard to go very fast. If you decide to try this event, make sure that you're entering a contest designed for beginners, and that you won't be going faster than you are ready to go.

Mogul Contests

Sometimes there's a fourth event in snowboarding contests: mogul riding. Moguls are the big bumps that form on the steep slopes at ski areas. Each mogul contestant is judged on four points: how closely he follows the fall line down the hill, how fast he goes, how many turns he can make in one run, and how many aerials he can do.

Mogul contests are very rare, however. Most are held at western ski areas, where there are more moguls

than on ski hills in the east. You also have to be a very good snowboarder to do well in mogul events. Most snowboarders don't enter mogul contests until they have at least a few years of experience.

How to Find Contests

The easiest way to find out about contests is to check out the snowboarding magazines. They publish lists of upcoming contests scheduled around the country. Usually these lists are toward the back of the magazines. Some contests may also be advertised.

Many ski areas also publicize upcoming snowboarding contests. Whenever you're snowboarding at a resort, check out the lodge and cafeteria for posters announcing upcoming contests.

You could also try contacting the American Snowboarding Federation, an organization that helps organize and promote competitions. If you have no luck finding a contest near you, write to the ASF at the address given in the Appendix at the end of this book and ask for information on contests in your area.

Bodyboarding is one of the easiest sports to compete in. Even though the sport is new, it's easy to find contests to enter. There are hundreds held every year around the country. At each, there are beginners who are competing for the first time. And there's usually no minimum age to enter, so it doesn't matter how young or inexperienced you are.

Jamborees

Before you enter a contest, consider learning more about bodyboarding at a "jamboree," which is sort of a class in bodyboarding. You get free instruction from top pro and amateur riders, and you get to try out different kinds of boards and fins and other equipment at no cost. And you have a chance at winning boards and other prizes in a raffle.

This off-the-lip maneuver has a bodyboarder grabbing air!

Each summer, the Morey Boogie Company—named after Tom Morey, the inventor of the modern bodyboard—sponsors jamborees around the country. The teachers are often some of the world's most famous riders.

Here's how a jamboree typically works: You can sign up in advance at a local surf shop, or you can enroll at the beginning of the jamboree. Most of the participants will probably be ordinary beach-goers who happened to be on the beach when the jamboree started and decided to give bodyboarding a try.

The jamboree starts with demonstrations by the teachers. Then the participants practice on the beach, where it's easier for the teachers to see what the students are doing and point out problems. Finally, the participants go into the water with the teachers and apply what they've learned on the beach.

Jamborees are usually held on Saturdays and Sundays. Sometimes they will include a day of competition in addition to a day of instruction. There are usually a dozen or so each summer on the beaches of California, Florida, North Carolina, Virginia, Maryland and Rhode Island. You don't even have to own a board and fins to participate—they are supplied at no cost.

You can find a jamboree near you by calling or writing Morey Boogie and asking for information on jamboree schedules. Or you can ask someone at a surf shop if he or she knows of one planned for your area soon.

Contests

If you miss out on a jamboree, don't worry. There are lots of bodyboarding contests to enter. Morey Boogie sponsors about 450 competitions every year. And that's just one sponsor! Other companies such as Scott Hawaii, BZ Bodyboards and Foam Design also hold bodyboarding contests.

You'll start out competing in the amateur division. There is usually no minimum age, and this group includes competitors as young as seven years old. Don't be afraid to enter a competition. There are novices in virtually every amateur contest.

Most competitions are split into a series of heats and rounds. One heat usually contains two to eight riders. The riders all go out into the water at once and compete at the same time. All are jockeying to catch the best waves. But courtesy is still the rule here, because if someone gets in another person's way, he or she is penalized by the judges.

Onshore, there is a panel of four to six judges, who may have seats up on a platform to see the water better. Sometimes the judges have "spotters" to help point out tricks done by riders.

Judges score riders on the number of tricks done in each ride and the distance of their rides. This forces bodyboarders to look for waves that give the longest rides and to do a lot of tricks in each ride. Riders who score highest move on to the next round. If there are lots of riders, there may be several preliminary rounds. Ultimately, the winner is decided in the final round, which includes only a handful of the best contestants.

How to Find Contests

Often bodyboarding contests are part of surfing competitions held by regional surfing associations, such as the Eastern Surfing Association, the Western Surfing Association, and the Texas Gulf Coast Surfing Association. All of these organizations are part of the United States Surfing Federation. To find a bodyboarding contest near you, write the USSF (listed in the Appendix) or one of the regional associations for a schedule of competitions.

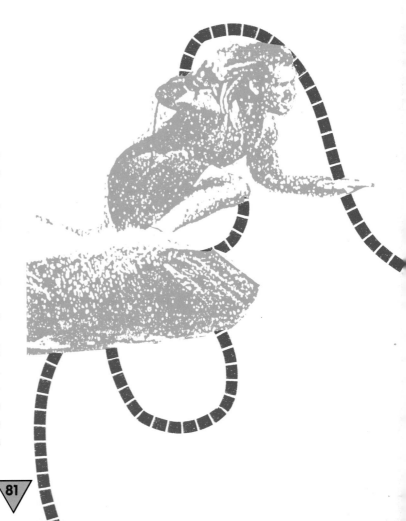

APPENDIX:

Here is a list of organizations and magazines which you can contact for more information.

Skateboarding

The National Skateboard Association
P.O. Box 1916
Vista, CA 92083
619-941-1844

Thrasher Magazine
High Speed Productions
Box 884570
San Francisco, CA 91488

Transworld Skateboarding Magazine
P.O. Box 6
Cardiff-by-the-Sea, CA 92007

Bodyboarding

The United States Surfing Federation
7104 Island Village Drive
Long Beach, CA 90803
213-596-7785

Eastern Surfing Association
11 Adams Point Road
Barrington, RI 02806
407-728-4325

Hawaii Surfing Association
c/o Anthony Guerrero
3107 Lincoln Avenue
Honolulu, HI 96816
808-737-0231

National Scholastic Surfing Association
P.O. Box 495
Huntington Beach, CA 92648
714-841-3254

Western Surfing Association
7104 Island Village Drive
Long Beach, CA 90803
408-662-4610

Body Boarding Magazine
P.O. Box 3010
San Clemente, CA 92672

For information on bodyboarding jamborees, contact:
Morey Boogie Bodyboards
2964 Oceanside Boulevard, Suite A
Oceanside, CA 92054
or call 619-439-0900 and ask for information on jamborees

Snowboarding

American Snowboarding Federation
P.O. Box 477
Vail, CO 81658
303-949-5710

New England Snowboarder
P.O. Box 468
Marblehead, MA 01945

Transworld Snowboarding Magazine
P.O. Box 6
Cardiff-by-the-Sea, CA 92007

Snowboarder Magazine
P.O. Box 1028
Dana Point, CA 92629

International Snowboard Magazine
P.O. Box 170309
San Francisco, CA 94117-0309

''Don't Pat the Dog''
(Chris Karol's snowboarding video)
send $25.95 to:
Motion Graphics
8340 S.W. 39th Avenue
Portland, OR 97219

GLOSSARY

Aggro—aggressive, wild, tough

Alpine—a style of snowboard riding which emphasizes speed and long graceful turns instead of the fancy tricks in freestyle riding

Barge—to make an aggressive move; a skateboarder who rides hard on a half-pipe ramp is said to "barge the ramp"

Bellyboard—the predecessor of the bodyboard: essentially a short surfboard constructed out of fiberglass and ridden in a prone, face-down position

Biffling—falling off a snowboard

Deck—the wooden surface of a skateboard on which the rider stands

Demo—short for "demonstration": For example, a snowboard that's for rent so that potential buyers can test it out

Durometer Scale—a number system for indicating the hardness of a skateboard wheel

El rollo—a corkscrew-shaped maneuver on a bodyboard in which the rider rolls completely over while riding a wave forward

Fakie—any snowboarding or skateboarding maneuver performed while the rider is moving backwards

Grommet—a bad or unskilled skateboarder

Flex—the flexibility of a snowboard or bodyboard

Freestyle—a style of skateboard, bodyboard and snowboard riding in which the rider does fancy jumps, twists and turns in no particular order

Gnarly—1) super good or hot; 2) extremely difficult or awful in appearance

Goofy-foot—a riding position on a radboard in which the right foot is forward

Gate—a pole stuck in the snow for snowboard riders to turn around in a slalom competition

Half-pipe—a U-shaped ramp for performing tricks made out of snow for snowboarders and wood for skateboarders

Kingpin—the bolt in a skateboard truck that allows the truck to be adjusted for flexibility

Leash—a cord that attaches a bodyboard or snowboard to its rider

Mogul—bumps on a snow or ski slope

Neoprene—a spongy type of rubber used to make wetsuits

Nose—the front end of a rad board

A 180—a 180-degree turn on a snowboard or skateboard in which the rider reverses direction

Paipo board—an ancient Hawaiian board made of wood and ridden like a bodyboard in a prone, face-down position

Rad—short for "radical": awesome, spectacular, fabulous, super cool

Rails—the side edges of a rad board

Reef break—a condition of the ocean in which the waves are breaking away from shore on a line of coral or rock

Shore break—a condition of the ocean in which the waves are breaking close to the shore, usually on a smooth and sandy bottom

Skeg—a plastic rudder that is sometimes added to the bottom of a bodyboard to lend stability

Slick skin—a vinyl coating added to a bodyboard to make it cut through the water better

Shredding—cutting back and forth on a mountain, hill, or wave on a rad board

Sidecut—the inward curve on the edge of a snowboard

Tail—the back end of a rad board

Truck—the metal assembly that holds the wheels and axles to a skateboard

Vert—short for "vertical": the top 12 to 18 inches of a half-pipe which is completely straight up and down

Wide point—the widest part of a bodyboard

Wipe out—when a wave hits you and you fall off your bodyboard

Photo Credits
J. Grant Brittain: 3, 10, 13, 17, 19, 20, 22, 26, 76
Jon Foster: 34, 37, 39, 60, 78
Guy Motil: 7, 35, 43, 47, 52
Buz Sipes: 5, 58, 62, 65, 66, 69, 80

About the Author

Ron King loves all sports, and he skis and competes in triathalons. As a kid, he was an excellent skateboarder, and as a teenager he became a radical surfer. Lately, King has become a big fan of the fast-growing sport of snow-boarding. He lives in Knoxville, Tennessee, where he edits Special Report sports magazine, and writes.